MALE AND FEMALE

HE

CREATED

THEM

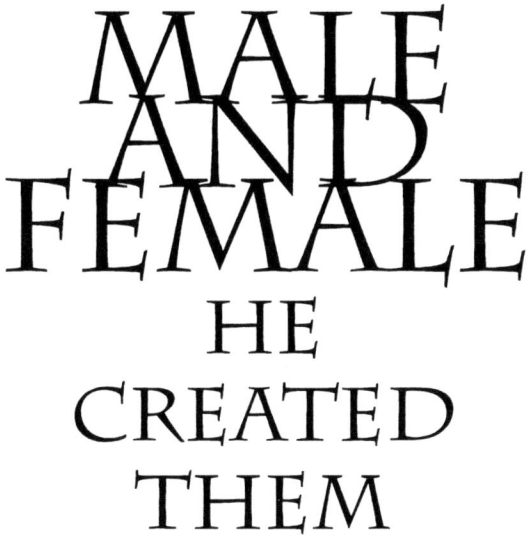

MALE AND FEMALE
HE
CREATED
THEM

YISRAEL BEN REUVEN

A Guide to Classical Torah Commentary
on the Roles and Natures of
Men and Women

TARGUM/FELDHEIM

First published 1996
Copyright © 1995 by Yisrael ben Reuven
ISBN 1-56871-096-8

The author is grateful for permission to use excerpts from the following works:
Judaism Eternal II and Horeb: Soncino Press
The Pentatuech: Judaica Press
The Hirsch Siddur and the Hirsch Haggadah: Feldheim Publishers
For Love of Torah: Mesorah Publications
Selected Speeches: CIS Publishers

Published by:
Targum Press Inc.
22700 W. Eleven Mile Rd.
Southfield, Mich. 48034

Distributed by:
Feldheim Publishers
200 Airport Executive Park
Nanuet, N.Y. 10954

Distributed in Israel by:
Targum Press Ltd.
POB 43170
Jerusalem 91430

Printed in Israel

Rabbi CHAIM P. SCHEINBERG

KIRYAT MATTERSDORF

PANIM MEIROT 2

JERUSALEM, ISRAEL

הרב חיים פנחס שייינברג

ראש ישיבת ״תורה אור״

ומורה הוראה דקרית מטרסדורף

ירושלים

מכתב המלצה

באתי לאסהודי אגברא, תולדותיהם
כיוצא בהם. ואף שאין דרכי להיות כמסכים
על ספרים מ״מ לא עמנה על ברכתי שיזכה
להרבות כבוד שמים על ידי ספרו על הענין
הנחן בזמנינו של תפקיד איש ואשה.
בברכה לתלמיד מרב

חיים פנחס שיינברג

פה עיה״ק ירושלים

RABBI REUVEN FEINSTEIN

ר"מ תפארת ירושלים ד'סטאטען אײלאנד

500C GRAND STREET
NEW YORK, N.Y. 10002

(212) 777-7935

לג' בעומר תשנ'ה

הנה ראיתי ספרו של הרב ישראל ... חבר הכולל ... בשם
Male and Female He Created Them. שהוא ביאור יסודי על פי תורתינו הקדושה
להסביר תפקידים מיוחדים של אנשים ונשים וכמה הם משונים במציאותם ממקורות
הראשונים ואחרונים.

יש בזמן הזה הרבה טועים ובונים בענין זה השקפות זרים ומזייפים דעת תורתינו
השפיעו על יריאים ושלימים לעשותם מבוכים בדעת בהבנת ענין זה.

המחבר עמל הרבה וכן חברי הכולל המסייעין אותו לברר ענין זה להסבירו
לרבים. יהי רצון שיהיה תועלת למבקשי האמת.

אני מברך אותו וחברי הכולל שיצליחו בכל מעשיהם לשם שמים בין ברוחניות
בין בגשמיות.

Contents

Preface 7

Introduction 9

Part One   **In God's Image**

One   To a Land Flowing with Milk and Honey 15

Two   The Wise Son 21

Three   Male and Female He Created Them 25

Part Two   **Man and Woman**

Four   The Beloved Companions 31

Five   The Exemption of Women from Positive Time-
             Bound Commandments: An Introduction . .51

Six   The Exemption According to the Talmud 55

Seven   The Exemption According to Rishonim 60

Eight   The Exemption According to Acharonim:
             The Maharal 76

Nine   Other Acharonim on the Exemption 94

Part Three   **Popular Misconceptions**

Ten   Popular Misconceptions: An Introduction 117

Eleven   The Rationalization and the Prohibition 121

Twelve   The Spiritual Natures of Men and Women 131

Thirteen   The Sin of the Golden Calf 157

Fourteen   The Last Creation 162

Fifteen   Avraham and Sarah .167

Sixteen   The Redemption from Egypt 177

Seventeen The Midrash on the Influence of Wives 181

Eighteen   Ramifications of the Misconceptions 197

Conclusion 217

Preface

This book focuses on three topics: the equality in worth of men and women and their equal opportunity for spiritual growth through their distinct roles in Jewish life, the derivation and reasons for the exemption of women from positive time-bound commandments, and the similarities and differences in the spiritual natures of men and women.

It is a small book, designed so that even a busy person can read it cover to cover. This is an important feature of the book. These complex subjects have been presented by our Sages with many paradoxical and counterbalancing statements and metaphors and, accordingly, a person needs a full range of commentary to build a balanced outlook. This book, while by no means encyclopedic, attempts to cover a fuller range of classical commentary than is commonly available in English literature on this subject. Such a range of material is necessary for proper handling of the subject.

As a word of caution, this book is not necessarily appropriate as an introduction to Torah for beginners. The material assumes some background in the principles of Torah learning and assumes also appreciation for Torah life. The endeavor here has been to present the beautiful wisdom of our Sages in a manner appropriate to current sensibilities. Nevertheless, some of the material may be too strong for a person with no Torah background. It may be as well not strong enough for others.

While the prose in this book is the product of a single writer, the ideas and selection of references are the work of a number of scholars. The author made hundreds of phone calls and trips to speak with experienced scholars and the leaders of our generation. Their input was more than suggestive. The author attempts to present this subject as it has been presented to him and had much assistance in doing so.

Along with the classical commentary, the author will offer his own thoughts on some of these matters and endeavor to name them as such. Usually the aforementioned thoughts will consist of questions on paradoxical statements amongst traditional sources, examination into ramifications of invalid teachings on the subject, and investigation into secular values which distance us from Torah true paths of living with regard to the roles and natures of men and women. Sometimes approaches will be suggested which may be helpful for grappling with the issues. Those suggestions, needless to say, are not definitive.

Much of the purpose of this book will have been fulfilled if the analyses and suggestions leave the reader with as many questions as answers. With Hashem's help, useful philosophical ideas and suggestions for behavior will be found in these pages; particularly in the classical sources contained here. But intrinsic to those ideas and suggestions should be an awareness of the subtlety of the material.

The author would like to end this preface with a prayer to Hashem that this book be truthful and constructive. This subject is often difficult to understand and to deal with. Additionally, the author asks the reader's patience with his shortcomings. His hope and the hope of those who contributed to the book is that one way or another the material here can be used to strengthen the *Avodas Hashem* and add to the general healthful living of those who read it.

Yisrael ben Reuven   PO. Box 1052
                                       Hightstown, NJ 08520

Introduction

The term "battle of the sexes" has had its application throughout history. Sadly, the human race has a propensity for unhealthy conflict and relationships between men and women seem to be fair game for this propensity. And as war between nations inflicts grave physical costs, reckless discord between men and women causes tragic spiritual costs. As the Midrash says, "When Israel is at peace among themselves, the divine presence will not depart from them."[1] Men and women need each other in innumerable ways, including the building of the homes and communities which are essential for everyone's divine service. Inter-gender conflict undermines this profound task. If one were to repeat this idea a million times, it would still not be emphasized enough.

Naturally, it is an understatement to say merely that Jewish men and women need each other. *Am Yisrael,* or the Nation of Israel, is like one being.[2] As the Arizal says, "Israel comprises a

1. *Midrash Rabbah, Vayikra* 26:2. The *Midrash,* which discusses social division caused by *lashon hara,* is used in the context of inter-gender conflict by Rav. S. Eisenblatt, *Chaim shel Osher,* vol. I (Jerusalem: Ma'ayan HaOsher Institute, 5741), p. 22. Translated into English as *Fulfillment in Marriage,* vol. I (Jerusalem: Ma'ayan HaOsher Institute, 5748), p. 25. (Rav Shmuel D. Eisenblatt, contemporary).
2. *Derech Hashem* 2:4:5 (Rav Moshe Chaim Luzzatto, b. 18th century).

mysterious single body."[3] Thus, we not only share a way of life and a national destiny, but we share existence. Our lives overlap. The *Reishis Chochmah* tells us that the souls of all Jews are bound together like the strands of a rope.[4] At the deepest levels we are all joined, so each person's loss is every person's loss,[5] each person's joy is every person's joy. Unhealthful conflict has no place in *Am Yisrael*.[6] While the first temple was destroyed because of idol worship, immorality, and bloodshed,[7] the second temple was destroyed because of baseless hatred between people.[8]

The Gemara tells us that a primary cause of the struggles between men and women can be found in the Hebrew words for man and woman. In Hebrew, the word for man is *ish*, and the word for woman *ishah*. Both words consist of the word for fire plus one of the letters of Hashem's name. The lesson is as follows: If you remove Hashem (the letters *yod* and *hei*) from the relationship between men and women, then you will only get fire, that is to say, conflict.[9]

It stands to reason that the situation worsens as time puts

---

3. *Likutei Torah, Taamei HaMitzvos* on *Vayikra* 19:18 (Rav Yitzchak ben Shlomo Luria, b. 16th century).
4. *Reishis Chochmah, Shaar HaYirah* 14 (Rav Eliyahu de Vidas, b. 16th century).
5. *Kuzari* 3:19 (Judah HaLevi, b. 12th century).
6. The *Mishnah* says: "By three things the world endures: truth, justice, and peace" (*Pirkei Avos* 1:18) and "Be of the disciples of Aaron, loving peace and pursuing peace" (*Pirkei Avos* 1:12).
7. *Yoma* 9b; Rav Eliyahu Dessler, *Michtav MeEliyahu*, (Committee for the Publication of the Writings of R. Dessler, 1964), 3:215.
8. *Yoma* 9b.
9. *Sotah* 17a as explained by *Rashi; Pirke d' R. Eliezer* as brought by Rav Samson Raphael Hirsch, *Judaism Eternal*, vol. II (New York: Soncino, 1976), p. 91.

years between society and the revelation of Torah at Mount Sinai. As Yesheyahu prophesied about the end of days, "And the people will be oppressed, person against person, neighbor against neighbor."[10] The secularization of the world seems to have run parallel with the explosion of marital problems. This should not be surprising.

What is equally troubling is that the strife between men and women has infected not only relationships between people but that of individuals and Hashem. The rhetoric generated by gender politics has produced massive confusion. People are unsure not only how to regard others but how to regard themselves. An instinctual feel for our own masculinity or femininity seems to evade many of us. We are either unsure or overly sure of how to conduct ourselves.

The Torah is here for us in such times of confusion. The myriad laws, stories, and philosophies of the Torah were written with the wisdom to carry us through the challenges of life. Hashem gave the Torah in His love for His people. Whatever is said here or elsewhere on these subjects can never refute the rule that Hashem wants the best for all of us. Accordingly, our discussion begins with an elaboration of that principle and its connection to our subject of the roles and natures of men and women in Torah.

---

10. *Yesheyahu* 3:5.

Part I

In God's Image

"God created man in His image. In the image of God, He created them, male and female He created them."

Bereishis 1:27

One

To a Land Flowing with Milk and Honey[11]

Hashem's creation of people was the culmination and underlying purpose of His creation of the universe.[12] In the words of the Ramchal, "The purpose of creation was for the Blessed One to bestow of His good to another."[13] Hashem created us in order to have recipients for his infinite generosity. We are here because Hashem loves us.[14]

Hashem's love is boundless.[15] As the verse says, "Hashem is good to all, His tender mercies rest upon all His works."[16] And

11. *Shemos* 3:8. The full section reads: "And the Lord said, 'I have surely seen the suffering of my people in Egypt. I have heard them cry out because of their taskmasters, for I know their sorrows. I will come down and deliver them from the hands of the Egyptians. I will bring them out of that land to a good, spacious land, to a land flowing with milk and honey' " (*Shemos* 3:7-8).
12. *Sanhedrin* 37a, 38a. See also *Michtav MeEliyahu* 3:292; *Mishlei* 10:25. For discussion in English, see *The Aryeh Kaplan Reader*: "Free Will and the Purpose of Creation," pp. 150-158.
13. *Derech Hashem* 1:2:1.
14. *Tehillim* 89:3.
15. *Yermeyahu* 31:2; *Midrash Tehillim* 119:21; *Tehillim* 136.
16. *Tehillim* 145:9.

we say twenty-six times each Shabbos, "His lovingkindness is eternal."[17] Each night we say, "With an eternal love You have loved the House of Israel."[18] If every person in the world were to suddenly become universally loving and caring, the love would in no way compare to that held by our Creator and Father in Heaven Who thinks about us and gives to us constantly.[19] For those who seek love, and who does not, the love exists in a magnitude of infinite proportions and a quality of unimaginable dimensions.[20]

Just as Hashem's love is infinite, so is his wisdom.[21] Imagine a person who was the world's leading expert in every aspect of physics, economics, music, literature, horticulture, engineering, and medicine. Imagine a person who knew every fact stored in every mind, book, and computer. Imagine this person to be also history's greatest composer, writer, athlete, chef, political leader, parent, and friend. As incredible as such a person would be, as famous and adored as this person would be, his wisdom and abilities would not compare in even the minutest degree to that of Hashem. We are as incapable of truly fathoming His wisdom[22] as we are incapable of truly fathoming His love.

In Hashem's infinite love, He does not want for us merely to experience a limited goodness. He wants for us the ultimate

---

17. *Sidur, Shacharis, Pesukei Dizimrah* from *Tehillim* 136.
18. *Sidur, Maariv, Ahavas Olam*. In *Nusach Ashkenaz* we say each morning, "With an unbounded love You have loved us Hashem."
19. Rav Bachya ben Asher, *Chovos HaLevavos, Shaar HaBitachon* 2:3 (Rav Bachya ben Asher, b. 14th century).
20. *Devarim* 10:15; *Chovos HaLevavos, Shaar HaBitachon* 2:3.
21. *Chovos HaLevavos, Shaar HaBitachon* 2:3; *Tehillim* 139:7-10; Rambam, *Moreh Nevuchim* 3:20.
22. *Shemos* 20:15-16; *Koheles* 7:23-24.

goodness.[23] Accordingly, in His infinite wisdom, He created the world so that people could use it to live in either a moral or an immoral fashion. By striving to live in a proper way, we earn our divine rewards. After earning them, we enjoy them without shame and in as high a degree as is possible for us.[24] It is a monumental and fulfilling challenge.

The challenge assumes many forms.[25] Sometimes our task is to overcome our inborn desire for physical indulgence.[26] Sometimes the task is to believe in the imperative and merits of the commandments despite persecution from other nations.[27] Every generation faces a unique set of tests.[28]

Our generation is challenged with, among other things, maintaining healthy social values despite the more negative influences of secular society. The world has always offered its

---

23. *Derech Hashem* 1:2:1.
24. *Derech Hashem* 1:2:1. See also *Meam Loez, Bereishis* 2:7. The experience is analogous to the satisfaction gained from earning a living. Prolonged and indulgent dependence on others for sustenance tends to diminish self-esteem. Self-reliance, with faith in Hashem, increases it. There are many angles from which to describe this process. One can say also that the greatest goodness in the universe is Hashem Himself. Our best course of life is to get as close to Him as is possible. He created the world and hid Himself in it in order to give us a challenge (*Derech Hashem* 1:2:1).
25. See *Pirkei Avos* 5:4.
26. *Derech Hashem* 1:4:3 and 1:4:6.
27. *Devarim* 4:25; Rav Bachya ben Asher, *Kad HaKemach, Emunah, d'h VeDavar yaduah*.
28. *Michtav MeEliyahu* 1:175. For discussion in English see Rabbi Aryeh Carmell, *Strive for Truth*, vol. II (New York: Feldheim, 1985), "The Unity Principle Through the Ages," pp. 231-234 (Rav Eliyahu Dessler, b. 19th century).

temptations. Many ancient cultures worshiped idols.[29] Others glorified physical strength and beauty.[30] Modern society, while guilty of some of these gross diversions from divine service, has been guilty as well of destructive experimentation in the realm of social interaction.[31]

Western culture, and particularly American culture in recent decades, has experimented wildly with the time-tested institutions of marriage, parenthood, and family. Sometimes the experimentation is intentional and sometimes it results from neglect. Either way, the magnitude and variety is staggering. In the United States, thirty percent of all children born in 1991 were born to parents out of wedlock. The figure in 1960 was five percent.[32] In many states, adoption of children is permitted by adults engaged in relationships forbidden by Torah law.[33] Each decade in the United States, marriages by the million are formed and dissolved with minimal forethought. For a period of about thirty years, motherhood, one of humankind's most revered and

---

29. Rambam, *Mishneh Torah, Hilchos Avodas Cochavim* 2:1 (Rav Moshe ben Maimon, b. 12th century); *Moreh Nevuchim* 1:36; 3:37, and 3:29.
30. *Judaism Eternal*, vol. II, pp. 190-192 (Rav Samson Raphael Hirsch, b. 19th century).
31. Chaim Dov Keller, Rosh Yeshiva of Telz, Chicago, address to the 70th Annual Convention of Agudah of America, from "Family Values: A Torah Perspective," *Jewish Observer*, Iyar 7573, pp. 5-11 (Rav Chaim Dov Keller, contemporary).
32. Department of Health and Human Services, National Center for Health Statistics, *Vital Statistics of the United States*, 1991, vol. 1., *Natality* (Washington, D.C: GPO, 1993) from William Bennett, *The Index of Leading Cultural Indicators* (New York: Simon and Schuster, 1994), p. 47.
33. *Rockland Journal News*, Sunday January 30, 1994, F Section, page 1; *USA Today*, Friday, July 29, 1994, "Custody Cases: Growing Pains."

essential occupations, was derided in many segments of society. One could fill buckets with the tears of older women who missed their opportunity to experience this ultimate of experiences. The movement against motherhood is waning, but many were seduced by it in its heyday. Certainly, our great-grandparents would be astonished by these activities.

The repercussions of this culture's social experimentation should be familiar to us all. Data suggest that approximately one-half of all marriages in the United States can be expected to end in divorce.[34] Accordingly, most American children born today will spend part of their childhood in a single-parent family.[35] Additionally, children in all strata of society suffer from parental neglect in such essential areas as the teaching of basic values, the expression of love, and the development of self-discipline. Add to the heap the myriad troubles of many families which stay together. Crime and substance abuse are rampant. So is stress.

As mentioned in the preface, this book shall offer some analyses of these social changes, but analyses are incidental. The most important task for a person is to keep focused on the proper path of living as outlined by the Torah.[36] The Torah's wisdom can guide us through the storms of any generation. The permanent placement of carrying handles on the ark symbolize this property of the Torah.[37] It speaks to all situations. It can guide us

---

34. *National Commission on Children, Just the Facts: A Summary of Recent Information on America's Children and Their Families* (Washington, DC, 1993) from *The Index of Leading Cultural Indicators*, p. 59.
35. David A. Hamburg, MD., *Today's Children, Creating a Future for a Generation in Crisis* (New York: Random House, 1992), p. 33.
36. *Koheles* 7:13.
37. Rav Samson Raphael Hirsch, *Collected Writings*, vol. III (New York: Feldheim, 1984), pp. 197-199.

through any challenge. The perseverance of Orthodox Jewish life through thirty-three centuries of history proves the point. However, one of our greatest challenges is to allow the Torah to help us. Hashem gave us the Torah to enable us to seek Him out and earn our precious place by His side. Accordingly, the Torah is designed for our benefit. It is here to uplift us and to better us.

But like a parent who seems unkind for making a child clean his or her room, the Torah is easily misunderstood. Sometimes it seems to rob us of all our pleasure. Sometimes it seems to rob us of our self-esteem, Heaven forbid. The Torah is here only to awaken within us the ultimate pleasure and the ultimate self-esteem. The Torah is for our own good, as we were told in the desert:

> And now, Israel, what does the Lord your God demand of you? Only this: to revere the Lord your God, to walk only in His paths, to love Him...keeping to the Lord's commandments and laws, which I enjoin upon you today, for your own good.[38]

Each of us is created in Hashem's image and the Torah will show us how. We are challenged to remember this. Hashem wants to bestow goodness upon us. That is the purpose of the universe. Our best course of action is to learn exactly the nature of His plan.

---

38. *Devarim* 10:12-13. See also *Devarim* 5:25-26: "The Lord said, 'Very good...If only they could always feel like this, to stand in such awe and be so eager to keep My commandments. It would be to their advantage.' " See *Sefer HaChinuch, Parshas Terumah, Mitzvah* 95.

Two

The Wise Son

It should be advantageous, before getting into the heart of our discussion about men and women in Torah, to say a few words about the nature of Torah study in general. As mentioned in the first chapter, Hashem's wisdom is totally unlike ours. Hashem's wisdom is infinitely deep, while ours is bounded by physical realities.[39] The Torah serves as a link between our finite understanding and the infinite wisdom of our Creator.[40] Our physical attachments and the inability of our minds to conceive of supra-rational truths inhibit our connection to Hashem whose ways are purely good and unselfish. The Torah gives us a glimpse into the divine wisdom. Accordingly, in our study of the eternal Torah, we are forever growing as individuals. The Torah increases and remakes our understanding.

To put it another way, proper Torah study increases and transforms knowledge so that even so-called basics of Torah take on invigorated meaning. This idea has been eloquently summarized in the expression: "The ultimate in knowledge is to

---

39. *Yesheyahu* 55:9; *Derech Hashem* 1:1:6; *Siddur, Shacharis, Layolam Yehay Adam.*
40. *Pirkei Avos* 1:1 and 6:1; *Tomar Devorah* 2; *Derech Hashem* 4:2:1.

see that one does not know."[41] This is not the same as ignorance. Rather, it is an informed realization of the subtlety of truth. It is a religious experience, a glimpse at the infinity of Hashem. Rav Samson Raphael Hirsch says, "The deeper one penetrates, the higher he will set his aims; the more one investigates the humbler he will become, and the more reverently he will bow before the sublimity of God's Torah."[42]

Despite this principle of Torah study, there is an alarming tendency by many people to oversimplify Torah principles. The tendency is all too human. It may also be a particular problem of the era. Perhaps we have been conditioned by a rapid-paced society whose members seem increasingly to lack the time and interest necessary for careful thought. During recent American presidential elections, jokes circulated about the "sound bites" through which candidates build their campaigns. Sound bites are brief encapsulations of ideas intended to win over impatient audiences. One presidential candidate is a this; the other is a that. Is it all so simple?

In the teaching of Torah principles it most assuredly is not that simple.[43] The Torah is infinite it its nuances of meaning.[44] It is in part for this reason that a person can study it forever. This applies as well to discussions about the nature of people. The Jewish soul is characterized by infinitudes of attributes.[45] It is a

---

41. *Akeidas Yitzchok, Bereishis, shaar* 6 (near the beginning) (Rav Yitzchok Arama, b. 15th century); Rav Yeruchum Levovitz, *Daas Chochmah Umussar* 1:90.

42. Rav Samson Raphael Hirsch, *The Hirsch Haggadah* (New York: Feldheim, 1988), p. 76.

43. See *Shabbos* 86b; *Hagigah* 15a; *Pirkei Avos* 1:11.

44. *Pirkei Avos* 5:22; *Eruvin* 54b.

45. Ramak, *Tomer Devorah* 1 (Rav Moshe Cordovero, b. 16th century); *Nefesh HaChaim* 1:6; Malbim on *Bereishis* 2:19-20.

serious mistake for a person to come along and profess generalities about the Torah view on men and women. Men are this; women are that. It is not so simple. Perhaps that is why the classical literature handles the matter as it does. The Gemara uses myriad explanations and metaphors to discuss the roles and natures of men and women. Why should we use a few simple sentences? Naturally, one certainly can arrive at useful understandings on these matters. Those in the Gemara that argue for the precedence of learning over doing explain that learning is greater because it leads to doing.[46] Accordingly, for the Torah to instruct us, we must be able to understand it on some level. One of the things we must understand, however, is the danger of oversimplification and overgeneralization.

This principle is symbolized in the Passover Haggadah at the reading of the four questions. According to the Maharal, the wise son's inquiry into the nature of the laws of *Pesach*[47] demonstrates his desire to increase his wisdom. For this reason, this son is called the *chocham,* or the wise one.[48] In other words, he is called the wise son not because of his scope of knowledge, but because he sought knowledge and posed thoughtful questions.

As mentioned in the preface, the reader hopefully will find in this book a reluctance to try and answer all the questions. We can live with questions, indeed we are invigorated by them. The

---

46. *Kiddushin* 40b.
47. "The wise son, what does he say? 'What are the testimonies, the statutes, and the laws that the Lord, our God has commanded you?' " (*Haggadah shel Pesach, Magid*).
48. Maharal, *Haggadah shel Pesach, Divrei Nagidim* (*The Four Questions*), *d'h Keneged daled banim* (Rav Yehudah Loeve, b. 16th century, Poland). The same interpretation is offered by *Meam Loez, Haggadah, The Four Questions.*

aim of this book is largely to point out what cannot be generalized about men and women. The author intends also to offer numerous applicable explanations of the subject, but endeavors to do so in a dynamic and questioning manner. It's a longer road in one sense, but shorter in the total picture of things. Shortcuts are often a terrific means to getting lost. Oftentimes, with shortcuts, one thinks he will arrive sooner but, Heaven forbid, never arrives at all.

Three

Male and Female He Created
Them

The first Torah reference to gender (ie,. to men and women
as distinct entities) appears in the description of the creation of
Adam. As a being made in Hashem's image, Adam was not created as a man but as a composite of a man and a woman.[49] As
the verse says: "And God created man in His image. In the
image of God, He created him, male and female He created
them."[50] Adam is referred to initially with the singular "him"
and subsequently with the plural "them." Accordingly, the word
"him" can be understood to indicate not only masculinity but
femininity as well. Adam, the being equipped to carry out
Hashem's mission for the world, was part male and part female.
Rav Samson Raphael Hirsch explains this as follows:

The change from singular to plural, which we have

---

49. *Eruvin* 18a; *Moreh Nevuchim* 3:4; Malbim on *Bereishis* 2:21;
    Meam Loez, Bereishis 2:21-2; *Zohar* 3:44; *Midrash Haneelam
    Zohar Chadash* 16 as brought by *Torah Shelaimah* on *Bereishis*
    2:21.
50. *Bereishis* 1:27. See Rav Hirsch on *Bereishis* 5:2.

tried to reproduce in our translation of this first mention of man and woman in the story of the creation, already indicates the full equality of status, nay, the inner unity between man and woman in the conception and the destiny of "man formed in the image of God." This term embraces both sexes. Only man and woman together make up the idea of "man", and God created both of them alike without intermediary, and with the same conscious effort of will power.[51]

Whatever anyone ever attempts to say about men and women, the irrefutable fact is that both are created in Hashem's image[52] and both are needed for the carrying out of Hashem's mission on earth.[53] As Rav Hirsch says, "Right from the beginning God reached "mankind" male and female, both equally Godly, of equal worth, neither more in the likeness of God than the other, both given the same blessing by God, both together given the name 'Adam.' "[54]

While specifying the equality in worth of men and women, the Torah goes on to describe in different terms the respective natures and responsibilities of men and women.[55] These differences shall be elaborated upon in the course of this book. The point for now is that the differences in nature and responsibility do not detract from the ultimate equality of men and women in their respective worth to Hashem and general opportunity for divine service. Hashem created the world as a place for people to serve Him and to grow spiritually.[56] In this regard, all people

---

51. *Judaism Eternal*, vol. II, p 51.
52. *Pirkei Avos* 3:14.
53. *Judaism Eternal*, vol. II, p. 95; Rav Hirsch on *Bereishis* 1:28 and 2:18.
54. Rav Hirsch on *Bereishis* 5:2.
55. See chapter four.
56. *Shabbos* 88a; *Derech Hashem* 1:2; *Pirkei Avos* 6:11.

are equal.

This idea of equal worth and opportunity through differing roles is seen in the lives of Moshe and Aaron. Each was born with his own personal strengths. Moshe was a leader[57] and a lawgiver.[58] Aaron was a peacemaker[59] and a communicator.[60] Rashi tells us that the occasional placement of Aaron's name before Moshe's in specific verses of the Torah is proof of their equality.[61] Moshe was Israel's greatest prophet[62] and had more direct contact with Hashem than anyone else.[63] Nevertheless, Moshe and Aaron were considered in fundamental respects as equals.

The Midrash explicitly applies this principle of ultimate equal worth and opportunity to the differing roles and men and women.

> I call heaven and earth to witness be...man or woman...only according to their actions will the spirit of holiness rest upon them.[64]

We see again that ultimate opportunity for spiritual endeavor is bound neither by our roles nor our natures. Certainly, heaven and earth know of the divinely prescribed roles and natures of men and women. Yet heaven and earth will testify that our actions determine our religious well-being.[65]

---

57. *Shemos* 18:18-25.
58. *Shemos* 35:1; *Pirkei Avos* 1:1.
59. *Pirkei Avos* 1:12.
60. *Shemos* 7:2; *Akeidas Yitzchok, Shemos, shaar* 35.
61. *Shemos* 6:26.
62. Rambam, *Sheloshah Asar Ikarim* 7.
63. *Devarim* 34:10.
64. *Seder Eliyahu Rabbah* 9. Also brought in *Judaism Eternal*, vol. II, p. 96.
65. In other words, ultimate spiritual accomplishment is not hindered by anyone's role or nature.

Part II

Man and Woman

"Desire what your Maker desires and rejoice in your portion, whether it be great or small. Entreat Him to lead your heart to follow His teachings. As for everything else, 'Cast upon Hashem your burden [and He will sustain you' *Tehillim* 55:23]."

Rabbeinu Asher: *Orchos Chaim* 69

"God has divided the sexes, giving each specific tasks in the fulfillment of life. Both tasks, if fulfilled in purity, are equally sublime, equally holy."

Rav Samson Raphael Hirsch: *Horeb* 433

Four

The Beloved Companions[66]

Notwithstanding the creation of Adam as male and female, the first man and woman, after the separation of Adam into two beings, are referred to by different names. He is called Adam,[67] and she, before the fall from Eden, is called Ishah[68] and afterwards is called Chava.[69] This distinction is significant given the tendency in Chumash for personal names to reveal essential information about their owners.[70] This applies in particular to names given by Adam, as Adam possessed a gift for seeing into the nature of things and ascribing appropriate names to them.[71]

---

66. *Sidur, Sheva Berachos, fifth blessing*: "Grant abundant happiness to the beloved companions as you gladdened your created being in the Garden of Eden from before time."
67. *Bereishis* 2:23.
68. *Bereishis* 2:23.
69. *Bereishis* 3:20.
70. See *Bereishis* 29:32-35 and 30:17-22; *Akeidas Yitzchok, Bereishis, shaar* 12; *Meam Loez, Bereishis* 3:20 and 4:16; Rav Hirsch on *Bereishis* 1:26 and 5:30-31.
71. *Bereishis* 2:20; *Meam Loez, Bereishis* 2:20; Rav Hirsch on *Bereishis* 2:20.

Rav Hirsch tells us that the name Adam is related to the word *edom,* or red. As the least broken color of the spectrum, red symbolizes the "nearest revelation of the divine on earth."[72] The name Adam is also related to *hadom* or footstool. As the footstool of the feet of the divine presence, man is the "transmitter and bearer of the glory of God on earth."[73]

The *Akeidas Yitzchok* tells us that while the woman is part of the concept of Adam, her names Ishah and Chava reveal the dual purposes by which she functions as part of Adam. These purposes are to be respectively a helpmate to her husband and a mother to her children.[74]

The *Akeidas Yitzchok* says also that the woman, like the man from whom she is formed, may utilize her mind to grasp matters of wisdom and piety. In doing so, she follows the example of the *Imahos* and of righteous women and prophetesses in Jewish history. This intellectual activity is a function of her role as Ishah. However, all of this applies only if she is true to her purpose of being a helpmate to her husband. As the *Akeidas Yitzchok* says, "In sum, the first name (Ishah) applies to her in accordance with her being a helpmate."[75]

This may follow from the fact that the woman's name Ishah[76] and the woman's intellectual capabilities[77] both come

---

72. Rav Hirsch on *Bereishis* 1:26.
73. Rav Hirsch on *Bereishis* 1:26.
74. *Akeidas Yitzchok, Bereishis, shaar* 9:7-8. *Chaim shel Osher* says that the obligation of women in a variety of commandments indicates through simple logic that general service to Hashem is a woman's purpose in life along with the specific functions of being a wife and mother (*Chaim shel Osher*, vol. II, p. 30). In *Fulfillment in Marriage*, vol. II, p. 25.
75. *Akeidas Yitzchok, Bereishis, shaar* 9:7-8.
76. *Bereishis* 2:23; *Akeidas Yitzchok, Bereishis, shaar* 9:7-8.
77. *Akeidas Yitzchok, Bereishis, shaar* 9:8.

about because she is taken from the Ish, or man. As the verses say, "It is not good for man to be alone. Let us make a helpmate with relation to him,"[78] and "And the rib which Hashem had taken from the man He built into a woman."[79] According to the *Akeidas Yitzchok*, since she was taken for the purpose of being a helpmate, she must act as a helpmate to retain the name and function of Ishah.

This idea of helpmate shall be elaborated upon later. It is important to stress now that this helpmate is neither servile nor inferior. Rav Hirsch has pointed out elsewhere that Sarah never refers to Avraham directly as "my lord." As Rav Hirsch says, "Jewish wedlock with its ultimate union of man and wife does not know of such a term of subjection."[80] He says also, "The Sages expect from the husband the most tender consideration and the most loving and respectful treatment for his wife."[81]

On the term "helpmate," Rav Hirsch explains as follows:

> "I will provide for him a help mate for him"...is that kind of assistance which through taking over a part of the work to be performed allows the other partner to concentrate his attention on the part which is left to him to perform, and so enables him to perform his part properly, thus securing the proper performance of the whole. This is the essence of the division of labour.[82]

Men and women are not in a contest with one another. Such would contradict Jewish sensibilities and would be impossible due to their differences. What would be the means of competi-

---

78. *Bereishis* 2:18.
79. *Bereishis* 2:18.
80. *Judaism Eternal*, vol. II, pp. 63-64.
81. *Judaism Eternal*, vol. II, p. 93.
82. *Judaism Eternal*, vol. II, p. 55.

tion between a singer and a computer programmer? Men and women are different from one another and by virtue of those differences have the potential for greater sum accomplishment.

An important feature of the differences in the roles of men in women is that they create an equality between them. Rav Hirsch explains:

> It places the woman forthwith on a footing of equality with the man, while giving to each a different sphere of activity, so that the man cannot fill the position of the woman nor the woman that of the man. Both stand and work on the same line, they play into one another's hands and by their co-operation consummate the human task. This partition of the human task is no mere matter of agreement, the woman has from the very beginning been created *kenegdo*, in the way required for such a fruitful supplementing of the man's activity.[83]

Thus, not only do the roles of men and women differ, but they are each invaluable to the mission of humankind. For these reasons, the two roles cannot be compared in any quantitative way. Neither is better than the other.

An important corollary of this principle is that the wife's assistance in the husband's endeavors succeeds only, as Rav Hirsch says, if the wife "does not work at what he is doing, but works opposite him. Were the other being a man, he himself would have all the obligations upon his own shoulders, and he would again need 'help.'"[84] And Rav Hirsch says also, "Because the wife is to be the *eizer* of her husband, she must be *kenegdo*;

---

83. *Judaism Eternal*, vol. II, p. 55.
84. Rav Hirsch on *Bereishis* 2:18.

because she is to complement him she must have *different* characteristics to his."[85]

It would probably be wise to offer some explanation at this point to the concepts of wife and mother, and following that, some explanation to the concepts behind the man's role. The dignity, value, and enjoyment of the roles of wife and mother have been under attack by some segments of society in recent decades, and the subject has become complicated for many people. Likewise, misinformation and reactionary prejudice surrounds this subject. As mentioned at the start, the Torah is written with divine love for all people. A person owes it to himself or herself to exercise openness, trust, and patience to see the humanity in Torah prescriptions for life. The one who flees from anything unfamiliar or uncomfortable dooms himself to mediocrity. It is reminiscent of the person who comes to the Passover seder rabid for food. He waits through the eating of the bitter herb, the breaking of the matzah, and the Haggadah. In a huff, he storms out, decrying his hosts who promised a meal and delivered bitter herbs. As the door slams behind him, the host brings out the meal.

Many teachers and writers have expended much energy trying to explain the fairness and humanity of the Torah in these matters. The author shall not attempt to repeat the many fine points made in this effort, only to present a few of his own. With Hashem's help, this additional angle on the subject will enhance proper understanding of the matter.

A primary cause of misunderstanding on this subject is that wifehood and motherhood are largely supportive and non-flashy roles, and Western culture tends to focus on the independently heroic and the conspicuous. This tendency is apparent in sports

---

85. Rav Hirsch on *Bereishis* 2:24.

culture where individuals receive praise earned by entire teams of players. Torah thought is not so concerned with newsmakers. It is fine if someone is called upon to be a leader, but the most satisfying and important paths of life are not assumed to be the most visible ones.

An example of this idea may be found in the story of Eliezer the servant of Avraham. Eliezer dedicated himself to finding a wife for Yitzchok, Avraham's son, even though he desired to have his own daughter married to Yitzchok.[86] Clearly, Eliezer worked in the service of Avraham and in the immense shadow of Avraham.[87] Nevertheless, the Chumash dedicates dozens of verses to give details of Eliezer's journey and even repeats his story.[88] One must note that the Chumash is written with extreme economy. An extra letter can be used as a source for fundamental laws.[89]

One may ask why is the work of this man in a supportive role to be considered as so important. One may answer that working in a supportive role is the highest task anyone can undertake. The whole mission of the Jewish people is to play a supportive role to Hashem in His plans for the world. When a husband goes off to learn Torah, he is going to study his role of

---

86. *Rashi* on *Bereishis* 24:39.
87. *Bereishis* 24:34.
88. *Bereishis* 24. See *Midrash Rabbah, Bereishis* 60:8, which says, "The ordinary conversation of the servants of the house of the Patriarchs is considered more important than the Torah given to their children. The explanation of Eliezer takes two or three pages and then it is repeated. The [law] of the creeping creature is one of the fundamentals of the Torah and yet the law of its blood and flesh defiling is [learned] from a hint in the verse."
89. *Midrash Rabbah, Bereishis* 60:8; *Akeidas Yitzchok; Bereishis, shaar* 22; *Meam Loez, Bereishis* 24:54.

servant to Hashem. It is not that the wife enables the man and the man goes yachting. The man goes to study what the Master of the Universe wants from the human race. We are all enablers; we are all servants. As the congregation chants out loud numerous times on Rosh Hashanah, "We are your servants, and you are our King."[90] The Ramchal expresses it as follows:

> The situation is similar to a household where each servant is appointed to a task appropriate to him. [Each servant] must fulfill his task in accordance with its terms so that the work and needs of the household can be completed.[91]

The exact form and timing of our respective contributions may differ, but the essence of these different contributions is of singular form. We are all children and servants of Hashem.

These points are largely alien to the constituents of contemporary culture. It would be difficult to explain to the secularly oriented person the Jewish commitment to serving Hashem. It would be hard to explain to a society obsessed with competition the Jewish feeling for teamwork. Notably, the non-Torah observant person of previous centuries and even early in this century often had an appreciation for concepts like duty and service. For example, public school education in the United States of the 1920s centered on the teaching of citizenship and civic service.[92] This civic service was not even remotely on the order of that of a Torah-centered society, but it was an expression of community involvement. It was for our purposes an example of how even secular society once cherished values like duty and team-

---

90. *Machzor Rosh Hashanah, Chazaras HaShatz, Musaf.*
91. Ramchal, *Mesillas Yisharim* 22.
92. Robert Reich, *The Next American Frontier* (New York: Penguin Books, 1983) pp. 55-56.

work.

We need group effort for real accomplishment. As mentioned earlier, men and women assume different roles so that, to apply a metaphor, the product of their efforts is greater than the sum of its parts.[93] Another metaphor for this is stereo music systems. In mono systems, each speaker plays the same sound as the other speaker. In stereo systems, the sounds coming out of each speaker differ, and the total sound is much fuller and richer than in a mono system. A third metaphor is the advanced economic system. The material success of the American economy is largely a function of specialization of job functions. Some people are engineers, and others are salespeople. Even the engineers specialize in different engineering applications. The collaboration of these specializations has produced the wealthiest economy in history — for better or worse. The availability of metaphors for this point regarding the power of specialization should show its reflection in the nature of life.

Another boon of the different roles for men and women is that it creates emotional closeness between them. If men and women were made alike, then their coming together would be bounded in intimacy. As differently made beings who depend upon one another, the coming together is much closer. In a sense, they may become as one being.[94] An apple tree and a pear tree standing together are just two trees in the same field. But a

---

93. *Judaism Eternal*, vol. II, p. 54.
94. Rav Hirsch says that two like beings tend to magnify one another's good and bad characteristics but do not complement one another. However, man and woman, as complementary beings, when united, "tend to produce the perfect being suitable to become perfectly the *basar echod* [being of one flesh]" (Rav Hirsch on *Bereishis* 2:25).

leaf and a fruit together comprise part of one tree. Their relationship enjoys more closeness.

Incidentally, the emphasis on a woman's duty as wife and mother should not be taken as a de-emphasis of the man's duties as husband and father. The man's obligations to his wife and children are clearly established throughout the Talmud.[95] People are central to divine service, and these are the people closest to him. Their happiness, development, and safety should be foremost to him. It is just that the man has additional primary functions such as learning Torah. Fittingly, the additional primary functions benefit his family.

A second hesitancy by some people to the Torah's emphasis on wifehood and motherhood as primary roles for most women stems from a perception of these occupations as being unfulfilling. The question would go as follows: Perhaps the contributions of the less conspicuous members of the team are as valuable as that of every other member. Still, is that less conspicuous role enjoyable?

One might be tempted to say simply that all paths of divine service are enjoyable by virtue of their being divine service. Serving Hashem is the ultimate pleasure. As the verse says, "Be not like servants who serve their master on the condition of receiving a reward."[96] Perhaps this principle can serve as a guideline for the subject. But another verse says, "Its ways are ways of pleasantness."[97] This latter verse implies that the Torah's prescriptions for living are written with sensitivity and

---

95. *Yevamos* 62b; *Baba Matzia* 59a. See chapter seventeen for more references.
96. *Pirkei Avos* 1:3 as explained by *Chovos HaLevavos, Shaar Avodas HaElokim* 3.
97. *Mishlei* 3:17.

understanding of the components of happiness. The idea of Torah is pleasant and the actual "ways" of the Torah are pleasant. With this said, one may ask: how are the roles of wifehood and motherhood pleasant?

To address this question, it may help to first propose an analysis as to why these roles have been misunderstood in our generation. Probably the bulk of the questions (or criticisms) concerning these roles have come from secular literature of the nineteen sixties and seventies. Prior to that time and possibly back to the beginning of time, these roles were givens in life and were not generally doubted or questioned. The secular literature on gender in the sixties talked about the staleness of housework in the late twentieth century suburban home and the possibility of career development for women as an antidote.

The Orthodox Jew is not surprised to hear about boredom and despair in the secular American suburban home. In such settings throughout most of the recent decades, the husband's chief goals were oftentimes to rise in occupational status and to bring home money for house improvement, vacations, and education for his children's occupational aspirations. The wife's goals oftentimes were to beautify the home and herself for beauty's sake, to help her husband to rise in occupational status, and to help the children along the same path.[98] Admittedly, parents may also have actively pursued the adherence to some moral code. This may have meant good citizenship or general non-Torah religious values. But this latter pursuit does not seem to have been in general anything more than an accompaniment or supplement to materialistic ambitions. The rapid decline in morality

---

98. In more recent years, occupational ambition seems to have become the singular focus of most families, i.e., the occupational ambition of every family member, each one focused on him or herself.

throughout American culture over recent decades indicates this dynamic. Moreover, suburban culture increasingly divorced itself from ethnic history, folklore, literature, community involvement, and even from family bonds. No wonder the housewife was often bored and frustrated. However, the problem was not the roles of wife and mother but the setting in secular suburban America.

It is often the case with secular social critiques that the critique is more worthwhile than the suggested remedy. For example, compare the depiction of the problems with capitalism to the suggested remedy of communism. On the matter of life direction for women, much popular literature of the sixties suggested careers for women. Has this worked? Admittedly, the matter is difficult to debate. How does one grade personal fulfillment? However, polls do show that most working women would prefer not to work.[99] This should not come as a profound revelation. The working life is difficult for most people. Hashem told Adam long ago that bread would be earned "by the sweat of your brow."[100] This does not mean that work is not rewarding or important, but does imply that it is by no means a panacea for contentment.

This idea may be especially relevant to the Orthodox Jew of today. Financial demands are intense, and the average Jewish person is more commonly pressed into lucrative jobs which are not necessarily conducive to personal development. He can be glad to do it as part of his precious life as an Orthodox Jew. But the work in and of itself is not his highest goal in life. Either

99. *Monitor*, an annual survey of Yankelovich Partners, as quoted in "Stay at home Moms Are Fashionable Again in Many Communities," *The Wall Street Journal*, July 23, 1993, p. 1. See also *Newsweek* 6/2/86.
100. *Bereishis* 3:19. See *Judaism Eternal*, vol. II, pp. 56-57.

way, the pressures of the working environment can be most unhealthful.

In his commentary to the Passover Haggadah, Rabbi Marcus Lehman discusses how in particular the working world can be unhealthful to women. He points out that one of the elements of slavery in Egypt was that women were given men's work and men were given women's work.[101] The assignment of tasks contrary to one's nature is slavery in itself. The material demands of the modern era, in forcing women into the working world, have produced similar hardships. He comments as follows:

> It drives not only the man out into the hostile world but also the woman, out of her domain, the home. The woman of the house, the wife, the mother of children, who should preserve and protect the spiritual and physical atmosphere of the home, who in this struggle for existence in the outside world, is so often trampled underfoot, she is being forced more and more onto the battlefield.... A luring catchphrase "the emancipation of women," has been invented for this grim necessity, which estranges the woman from her actual vocation and places her in a position that is contrary to Nature; and her abandonment of the narrow but satisfying domestic round, and entry into the ranks of the fighters, is represented as an honor and recognition that had previously been denied to women. It has created the problem of "equality of the sexes" which imposes on women the burdens of life meant to be borne by men yet accuses of having an overbearing attitude, those who, while they acknowledge the complete equality of birth of men and women, yet wish those limits to be

---

101. *Sotah* 11.

respected that God has drawn through nature, sex, and temperament.[102]

Rabbi Lehman adds that the excessive focus on the struggle for existence and the inclusion of women in that struggle causes social problems. As he says, "Indifference, and overstrain, oversensitiveness and the whole range of nervous disorders that are described in short as neuroses, are new ailments of our times and were hardly known in former days. Whence do they originate, if not from the struggle for existence that corrodes the whole force of life; and the abnormal nature of that struggle is nowhere more clearly seen than in the participation in it of women."[103]

Besides all this, many women complain that their careers interfere with their family lives. Additionally, millions of children return home from school to households devoid of any parental contact since both parents are working. Careers for women have not been anyone's simple solution.

It is important to note that Orthodox Jewish women are not halachically prohibited from having careers and certainly not from taking jobs.[104] Whether or not a woman is obligated to be married is a matter of dispute amongst the *poskim*. The Rambam says that a woman is not commanded to marry in the strict sense

---

102. Rabbi Marcus Lehman, *Lehman's Passover Haggadah* (New York: The Gateshead Foundation for Torah, 1974), pp. 115-116.

103. *Lehman's Passover Haggadah*, p.116; *Chaim shel Osher* (vol. II, pp. 163-164) points out that high levels of nervousness in many women today are a negative manifestation of a natural tranquility within women. As often found in Torah thought, a person's greatest positive points can manifest as his most conspicuous personality deficits, Heaven forbid (*Fulfillment in Marriage*, vol. II, pp. 147-148).

104. *Maharam Shick* on *Shulchan Aruch, Orach Chaim* 163 discusses the merits of guiding one's daughter towards an occupation suitable for a Jewish woman (*Halichos Bas Yisrael* 10:6).

of the word[105] but she is strongly advised to do so.[106] The Ran says that a woman is commanded to marry.[107] Either way, a married woman is required to make her family her first priority. Appropriately, the nature of all but a few women is such that family life is their fundamental path to fulfillment.[108]

Naturally, it is difficult to gauge the joy foregone by women who do not focus on their roles as wives and mothers. How do you ask people to grade an experience they have never known? But the Orthodox Jewish woman knows. She knows the joy of caring for others. As the Talmud says, "More than the baby calf likes to drink, the cow likes to give milk."[109] While the self-interest orientation of capitalism may lead people to think other-

---

105. *Mishneh Torah, Hilchos Isurei Biah* 21:26; *Sefer HaChinuch* says that women are not obligated in the commandment of "be fruitful and multiply" (*Sefer HaChinuch, Mitzvah 1*). The *Meshech Chochmah* explains that childbirth may endanger a woman's life and accordingly cannot be imposed on her as a religious obligation (*Meshech Chochmah, Bereishis* 9:1).

106. Rambam speaks about the need for a woman to marry (*Mishneh Torah, Hilchos Isurei Biah* 21:26). Rav Hirsch calls motherhood "the true and highest vocation of woman" (*Judaism Eternal*, vol. II, p. 76).

107. *Tshuvos HaRan* 32 as brought by *Aitzei Orzim* 1:17 (*Otzair HaPoskim, Even HaEzer, Hilchos Priah U'Raviah* 1:17). The Ran says that when a woman marries she is fulfilling a commandment. This fulfillment is not as strong as other positive commandments, however, it is stronger than a *kiyum mitzvah*. The distinction is evidenced in the fact that she could nullify a vow made in public in order to fulfill this commandment (Rav Nissim ben Reuven, b. 13th century).

108. Rav Hirsch says, "there is no higher happiness for a woman than to have children" (Rav Hirsch on *Bereishis* 3:16).

109. *Pesachim* 112a.

wise, the fact remains that the greatest joys in life are from giving. Assuredly the joy of giving is subtler than the superficial thrill of self-interest, but is not that the whole point? Godliness is sublime as is true happiness.

It is important to note as well that role of the Jewish man is also orientated toward giving; although the channels differ sometimes from those of the Jewish woman. As Rav Hirsch explains, the male is the bearer of the spiritual tradition across the generations.[110] This is a form of giving. He also contributes to his community and supports his family in its moral, emotional, and financial needs. The woman's route for giving centers around wifehood and motherhood.[111] Interestingly, a number of female gender activists have publicly expressed their feelings on the joys of motherhood and expressed regret for not having had more children.[112] The Orthodox Jewish woman is fortunate to know well the immense personal satisfaction which comes from motherhood.

The Jewish woman also knows the feeling of being surrounded not by competitive coworkers but by family who trust her and need her. Office culture in the increasingly competitive American economy can be soul-deadening. Whom can one trust? In whom can one confide? And the friends one finds may not be around long given the mobility of the American worker. Layoffs, transfers, and career changes put thousands of miles between friends and make friend-seeking a perpetual quest. The Jewish woman normally has her family for a lifetime. The relationships have the potential to grow stronger by the year.

---

110. *Judaism Eternal*, vol. II. p. 51.
111. *Judaism Eternal*, vol. II, pp. 56-57.
112. See, for example, "Susan Sontag's unlikely bestseller," *Boston Globe*, Thursday, September 10, 1992, Living Arts section, p. 85.

As for fun and challenge, the Jewish woman daily experiences the laughter and play of children and uses her heart and mind to help them grow and to enjoy them. There is a large quantity of writings by Jewish and non-Jewish women about the joys and challenges of wifehood and motherhood. The author lacks the time and ability to recreate all of it here. But he wishes he could because it is so often inspirational and humbling.[113]

A third common source of resistance to the roles of wife and mother stems from vague feelings of loyalty and connection by some people to secular political movements and ideology. Some women, particularly those with more exposure to the secular world, experienced through the feminist movement their first expression of rebellion against the prevailing secular culture. Indeed, the Jews can be regarded as rebels against secular culture, and this experience of searching and challenging has its use. The problem is that much of the feminist movement, particularly that found in the popular press and university women's studies departments, is these days generally as secularized and vacuous as the society it alleges to oppose. Some occasional constructive insights notwithstanding, secular movements in general lack the altruism and breadth of understanding to provide entire life outlooks for people. Fortunately, much secular literature of recent years has examined the glaring problems of contemporary feminism. Much of it is written by women and read widely by an appreciative public.[114]

As a note, this discussion is addressed to both men and

---

113. See, for example, *More of Our Lives: An Anthology of Jewish Women's Writings*, ed. Sarah Shapiro (Jerusalem: Targum, 1993); Ruchama Shain, *Dearest Children* (New York: Feldheim, 1992); Mindy Gross, *How Long the Night* (Jerusalem: Targum, 1991).

114. See, for example, Phyllis Schlafly, *The Power of the Positive Woman* (New York: Jove/HBJ, 1977); Christina Hoff Sommers,

women who have lost sight of the Torah's general prescriptions for family life. We all must come to appreciate the role of wife and mother as the Torah appreciates it. The men who push their wives into careers for increased discretionary income at the expense of family life are making a tragic mistake; likewise the people who offer only token recognition of this world's dependence on the devoted wife and mother. Rav Hirsch has explained that Hashem made man and woman different from one another and did so with love and wisdom. As our natures differ so do our roles. As our natures are designed in "Hashem's image," so too, our roles bear divine worth. To fight this is folly.

Alternatively, some people ask for an explanation to why the man must be burdened with the more conspicuous religious obligations and the often unnerving financial obligations of supporting a Jewish family. It is not easy to shoulder the role of leader and provider. Responsibility for others can wear down a person. It demands seriousness and toughness. The questioner is advised, as with the questions regarding the women's role, to remember that any seeming inhumanness in the men's role has been shaped by secular materialistic values. The pressure to become educationally superior to others, to be an expert in all matters, or to succeed financially is borne from secular culture. The Torah does not ask the Jewish man to make that kind of a mark on the world. It is incumbent on him only to apply himself to Torah learning and to the financial support of his family to the best of his ability. He is not a workhorse for his family's indulgences as is so often the case in secular culture. While he works

---

Who Stole Feminism? (New York: Simon and Schuster, 1994); Warren Farrell, *The Myth of Male Power* (New York: Berkely Books, 1993). These are secular books which necessarily must be read with discernment, but they offer nevertheless valuable critiques of popular gender movements.

at his learning, by no means an easy undertaking, his wife works in her realm. They are both full-time workers, although in different spheres of activity.

What has to be discussed also is modern society's loss of appreciation for the contributions of fatherhood to the public good. People will speak somewhat of their respect for the responsible father, but they will more often broadcast their admiration for the millionaire and the professional with glamorous credentials or even the award-winning scientist or writer. Both men and women are guilty of this confusion of priorities. The resulting applause for the conquerors of material prizes and accolades drowns out the laughter of healthy families who are blessed with dedicated husbands and fathers.

Moreover, as Rav Hirsch explains, the contributions of fathers are essential to the development of children and to the building of society.

> The mitzvah of education devolves upon the father, whom God has endowed with the necessary abilities. Where a father neglects the duty, no other means can compensate. All the textbooks, all the teaching aids that have been invented as surrogates for the consecration of our youth in the home, will be of no avail.[115]

Maybe there is some praise due to the executive with the efficient department or the activist who turned around the educational program of his school district. But does any of this compare to the man who brings children into the world and who teaches these children the ways of dignity, compassion, and truth — the ways of the Torah. And later these children grow into adulthood and themselves raise children to fear and love

---

115. Rav Hirsch, *Hirsch Haggadah, Four Questions*: "As for the son who does not know how to ask," p.87.

Hashem, to care for their fellow, and to demonstrate the intrinsic rewards of Torah life. Fatherhood is a much more comprehensive and enduring undertaking than is careerism.

What is drowned out as well in the crowd's roar for conquering men is the delight of fatherhood. Surely, the rewards of family life emerge more discreetly and gradually than those of the career track. Children develop slowly and seem to respond as much to the dictates of their own natures as to that of a parent. The husband to a pregnant wife and father to eight children is neither free to roam the world nor to paint a masterpiece. But is there a greater adventure than sharing the world of another person and nurturing the development of people? Similarly, is there a greater adventure than the journey into one's deep need to care for another and to be committed to another? The world-traveling bachelor may have expressed parts of his psyche, but the deeper holds of his soul will be stagnant without the experience of fatherhood. Jewish men historically have been wise to the difference. Of course, the man or woman who is not blessed with children despite his or her efforts to have them is not counted in that group that deprived themselves. The desire and attempt to be parents are the essential ingredients of this experience and are well transferred to other avenues of care and commitment for others.

And what about a man's obligations in Torah study? Is this not an overwhelming request, to fill one's spare moments with toil and diligence? But again, it is the world at large which fails to understand the life of religious calling. Deep in the heart of man is a desire for service of Hashem.[116] It is a desire greater than that of indolence and luxury. Thus, the person not engaged in such toil for Hashem is the person with no peace. The obliga-

116. Chofetz Chaim, *Sefer HaMitvos HaKatzar, Hakdamah* (Rav Yisroel Meir HaKohen, b. 19th century).

tion of Torah learning may seem at first a foe to a man's dreams, but it becomes an ultimate dream to those who stay the course.

For both men and women the rewards of being a dedicated spouse are also underappreciated in today's society. This is the era of the personal development movement and the mid-life career change. But is it not also personal development to grow in appreciation for one's life-mate? Is it not an adventure as well to share the world of another person even when that world becomes familiar and predictable. The life of the Jew is a gripping drama; even our boredom is a fascinating subject given the import of our mission on earth and our inborn potential for goodness and spiritual striving. Arguably, the marital troubles of so many people today have come about because so much of society has lost its interest in and appreciation of people. But Jewish life is built around people. The men and women who are sensitized to this ethic will find that marital life according to the Torah offers rewards that grow more fulfilling over time.

Five

The Exemption of Women from Positive Time-Bound Commandments: An Introduction

Men and women are equally responsible for the great majority of the basic precepts of the Torah.[117] Some examples are the precepts concerning Shabbos,[118] Kashrus,[119] honesty in business,[120] proper speech,[121] performance of acts of kindness,[122] fear[123] and love[124] of Hashem, respect for Torah scholars,[125]

---

117. That is to say, precepts which are incumbent in regular circumstances. There are a large number of commandments which apply to individuals in special circumstances, such as the King and the Priests. Most Jews, whether men or women, are exempt from these commandments. See *Sifri, Bamidbar* 2 and *Kiddushin* 35a.
118. *Sefer HaMitzvos HaKatzar M'A* 19 and 20.
119. *Sefer HaMitzvos HaKatzar, M'LS* 86-100.
120. *Sefer HaMitzvos HaKatzar, M'LS* 34.
121. *Sefer HaMitzvos HaKatzar, M'LS* 77.
122. *Sefer HaMitzvos HaKatzar, M'A* 6; *Mishnah Peah* 1:1.
123. *Sefer HaMitzvos HaKatzar, M'A* 4.
124. *Sefer HaMitzvos HaKatzar, M'A* 3.
125. *Sefer HaMitzvos HaKatzar, M'A* 16 and 17.

truthfulness,[126] and carrying oneself with humility and dignity.[127]

The positive time-bound commandments are a group of a few commandments of which most are incumbent only on men. These commandments, such as Tefellin, are dependent on time to trigger their requirement.[128] Tefellin must be worn only in daytime and cannot be worn on Shabbos. The commandment of Tefellin is thus bound by time unlike the commandment of belief in Hashem.[129] One can work to develop his belief in Hashem at any time

In recent decades, the positive time-bound commandments have been subject to much discussion in certain segments of the Jewish world. Some women have felt insulted or short-changed by their legal exemption from these commandments. As mentioned earlier, women are assigned different responsibilities, such as childrearing, which are tremendously purposeful and challenging.

It would probably be unfair to say that one's discomfort with the disparity in assignment of commandments is always a case of seeing the grass greener on the other side of the fence; although that common human failing, as well as others such as jealousy or covetousness, Heaven forbid, may be the operative factor in many cases. Rather, blowing the Shofar and wearing

---

126. The *Mishnah* says, "The world endures on three things: justice, truth, and peace (*Pirkei Avos* 1:18).
127. *Sefer HaMitzvos HaKatzar, M'A* 6; *Kitzur Shulchan Aruch* 1:3; *Pirkei Avos* 5:24.
128. Other examples include Lulav, Sukkah, and *Krias Shema*. See *Kiddushin* 34a; *Tosefta, Kiddushin* 1:10. Exceptions to the exemption include the Eating of Matzah on Passover and the Kiddush on Shabbos (*Sefer Abudraham, Seder Tefillas shel Chol, Birchas HaMitzvos U'Mishpatim*).
129. *Sefer HaMitzvos HaKatzar M'A* 1.

Tzitzis and Tefellin are not only highly visible activities, but are pillars of Jewish life. To a participant of contemporary Western culture, the lack of primary involvement with the more conspicuous activities of life can be disconcerting.

To understand this, it helps to understand Western culture. As mentioned before, the United States and much of the Western World are socially mobile societies, where a primary ethic is self-reliance, and the prevailing cultural focus is on fame and wealth. The compensation for materialistic disparity is that equal opportunity is allegedly available to everyone. Naturally, the entire culture does not work that way, but plenty of it does, particularly in urban middle-class society where most Jews are reared. Since the focus in these cultures is less on regular living and the subtle beauty of life and more on the loud and conspicuous, it is understandable how some people could be confused by the assignment of the more visible commandments to men. It is as if women are being kept out of the action, so to speak.

Alternatively, some men have felt overburdened by their obligation in these commandments. The positive time-bound commandments by their very nature as being time-bound constrain a person. The commandment of *Krias Shema*[130] forces a man to awake early every day of his life. Of course, all people are generally obligated to rise early in the morning and to spend their time wisely. But this general obligation manifests itself differently in the specific commandments for each gender. The obligation for women is less explicitly outlined in terms of commandments.

Furthermore, some men have expressed discomfort and con-

---

130. This commandment requires the recitation of three paragraphs of Scripture twice each day. The first recitation must be made by the third hour of the morning, and the second must come at night (*Sefer HaMitzvos HaKatzar, M'A* 11).

fusion with the general assignment to women of many activities related to *chesed,* or acts of lovingkindness, for example child-drearing. While the halachah gives room for many individual predilections in these areas, requirements such as attending *minyanim* will take a man away from certain acts of *chesed* which can be performed by his wife. Some men have expressed that they gain a more complete religious feeling from performing the acts of *chesed* than from fulfilling the halachically mandated activities. Accordingly, these men, much like the women mentioned earlier, feel as if they are being kept from religious activity with which they would prefer to be involved.

Coming to understand why the halachah distinguishes between men and women can be a long journey, particularly for a person steeped in secular culture. Developing an appreciation for the differences and even a feeling of inspiration by them may take even longer; although such appreciation is definitely achievable.

As these journeys are often of a very personal nature, one cannot write the magic words that make everything understandable to everyone. The approach here will be to discuss the halachic nature of the exemption, the explanations given by classical commentaries, and to suggest new outlooks. Hopefully, the latter will be in line with Torah sensibilities and careful with sensitivities created by prevailing cultural forces of the day.

As a point of reference on these general subjects, it may be useful to repeat the idea that the Torah is, of course, written with infinite love for men and women and affords equal opportunity for divine service; although the paths of service may differ to some extent.

Six

The Exemption According to the Talmud

The discussion in chapter two about the limitations of human wisdom is especially relevant to the search for reasons for the exemption of women from positive time-bound commandments. This exemption is learned strictly from an hermeneutical technique given at Mount Sinai.[131] The derivation of the exemption is done by logical means, but the practical and philosophical reasons for the exemption are ultimately a mystery to us. In general, we can gain substantial philosophical insight into the reasons for commandments. However, ultimate reasons for the commandments are beyond our understanding. While the nonultimate reasons for some commandments, such as the prohibition against murder, are more easily understood,[132] the practical and philosophical reasons for other commandments, such as the prohibition against wearing clothing composed of linen mixed with wool and to a lesser extent the exemption of women

---

131. *Kiddushin* 29a; *Torah Temimah, Shemos* 13:9.
132. Rambam, *Moreh Nevuchim*, 3:26; *Sefer HaChinuch, Igeres HaMechaver; Igeres Moshe, Orach Chaim* IV, 49.

from positive time-bound commandments, are much less clear.[133]

The Talmud derives the exemption from the language and positioning of a series of verses concerning Tefellin and *Limud Torah*.[134] As said, the derivation is purely technical. The derivation is also not subject to disagreement in the Talmud. Unknown to many people is the fact that the Talmud does not discuss the practical and philosophical reasons for the exemption. In other words, the Talmud does not directly address the subject.

It may be useful here to discuss briefly the nature of *Chukim* or commandments whose reasons are not apparent to us. These *Chukim* contrast with *Mishpatim*, or commandments whose reasons can be grasped by human intellect. Rav Eliyahu Dessler writes that while *Chukim* are ultimately incomprehensible to the intellect, they can be appreciated though *deveikus,* or closeness to Hashem. The study of reasons for commandments is a primary source of inducing this emotional closeness to Hashem. Rav Dessler says that ironically, the closer we get to Hashem, the less we feel a need to hear reasons for His commandments. This is the idea behind the statement that Moshe Rabbeinu understood the reasons for all the commandments. His *deveikus* was extraordinary enough to render his appreciation for the *Chukim* equal to that of his appreciation for the *Mishpatim*.[135]

In this author's opinion, this system of *Chukim* and *Mishpatim* is part of what enables Torah to be a religion of the mind and the heart. Historically, Eastern cultures have tended to

---

133. Rav Moshe Feinstein, *Igeres Moshe, Orach Chaim* IV, 49 (Rav Moshe Feinstein, b. 19th century). For commentary on the elusiveness of reasons in general, see *Kasav Sofer, She'elos U'Tshuvos, Orach Chaim, Tshuvah* 75, *d'h L'mayshivas.*
134. *Kiddushin* 29a.
135. *Michtav MeEliyahu* 1:218-220.

stress transcendence of the mind, and Western cultures have tended to stress rational thought.[136] Torah combines the two to utilize both of these human strengths. Arguably, the restrictions of non-Torah religions to either the mystical, emotional, or logical realms render those religions ineffective in all of those realms. Accordingly, it is not a put-off to say that the reason for the exemption of women from positive time-bound commandments is ultimately unknowable. Rather, it is a fact of a religious system designed to develop the complete person.

The *Chukim*, although mysterious to us, are designed for our benefit. The Rambam elaborates on the importance of one's trust in the authority and benefit of the *Chukim*.

> Come and see how strict the Torah is about *Me 'ilah*. And what are these but wood and stones, dust and ash. Since the name of the Lord of the world is called upon them, they become sanctified. All who act in a profane manner with them have misappropriated them. Even if this act was unintentional, he is required to bring atonement. So all the more so by commandments that the Holy One Blessed Be He enacted for us, that a man should not reject them because he does not know their reason. And he should not apply to them things that are not correct about Hashem, may He be blessed, and not think of them with secular thoughts.

> Behold the Torah says, "And you should guard all My *Chukim* and all my *Mishpatim* and do them."[137] And the [Rabbis] may their memory be blessed, said that

---

136. For discussion of the Western rational tradition, see *Judaism Eternal*, vol. II, "Hellenism, Judaism, and Rome," pp. 187-209.
137. *Vayikra* 19:37.

this is to make observance and action apply to *Chukim* as well as to *Mishpatim*.[138] And by "action" is meant that one will do the *Chukim*. And by "observance" is meant that one will be watchful of them and will not regard them as inferior to the *Mishpatim*.

The *Mishpatim*, these are commandments whose reason is revealed and whose worldly benefit in doing them is known, for example stealing and spilling of blood [murder] and honoring one's father and mother. The *Chukim*, these are commandments whose reason is unknown. The Sages, may their memory be blessed, said, "[Hashem said] '*Chukim* I enacted for you, and you are not permitted to have negative thoughts about them.' " The evil inclination of man troubles him about them. And the nations of the world ridicule them, for example, the prohibition of eating the meat of the pig and of [mixing] meat with milk, and the [laws of] the heifer with the broken neck and the red heifer and the goat which is sent off.

How much David the King, may peace be upon him, was troubled by the heretics and idol worshippers who ridiculed the *Chukim*. And all the time that they pursued him with their false retorts that resulted from the limitations of the human mind, he would respond by increasing his attachment to Torah, as it is said, "The proudly rebellious have slandered me with a lie, but with my whole heart I will keep your precepts."[139] And it says there [also], "All your commandments are trust-

---

138. *Sifra* on *Vayikra* 19:37.
139. *Tehillim* 119:69.

worthy. They [scoffers] persecute me wrongfully. Help me."[140]

All the sacrifices are in the category of the *Chukim*. And the Sages said that the world endures on account of the service of the sacrifices. By doing the *Chukim* and the *Mishpatim*, upright people merit the life of the world to come. And the Torah places the command for the *Chukim* [before that of the *Mishpatim*] as it says, "Guard My *Chukim* and My *Mishpatim*, which if a person does, he shall live in them."[141, 142]

---

140. *Tehillim* 119:86.
141. *Vayikra* 18:5.
142. *Mishneh Torah, Hilchos Meilah* 8:8.

Seven

The Exemption According to Rishonim

As said earlier, the reasons for the *Chukim* by definition evade our ultimate logical grasp, but we are able to achieve some insight into some of them. The commandment of the Red Heifer totally evades our understanding.[143] But the exemption of women from positive time-bound commandments is a halachic reality whose reasons can yield somewhat to scholarly examination.[144] A number of Rishonim discuss the exemption; although their views bear close resemblance to one another.

Perhaps the most frequently stated explanation is that of the Abudraham. He explains that women are exempt from these commandments in order to free women to assume the responsibility of raising children.[145] The positive time-bound commandments impose time constraints which do not coordinate well

---

143. *Bamidbar Rabbah, Chukas* 19:3 as brought by *Michtav MeEliyahu* 1:218-220.
144. *Igeres Moshe, Orach Chaim* IV, 49.
145. *Sefer Abudraham, Seder Tefillas shel Chol, Birchas HaMitzvos U'Mishpatim, d'h VeKol Yisrael chaiyaveen.* (Rav David ben Yosef Abudraham, b. 13th century).

with the management of a household. Of particular relevance are the haphazard activities of children. A three year old child, for example, would tend not to wait for a mother to finish morning prayers before knocking the dishes off the kitchen table.

One may ask why the husband and wife do not share responsibility for these household tasks and the time-bound commandments. To this question, one is referred to the discussion in chapter four on the division of labor in the Jewish home. The man and the woman are assigned differing primary functions.[146] This social "division of labor" works to benefit everybody by allowing greater total accomplishment and a richer life. It would be social chaos if both husband and wife were obligated in the positive time-bound commandments. Somebody has to maintain the home and take care of the children who, needless to say, would be unable to fend for themselves while the parents are out performing the positive time-bound commandments.[147] According to the Abarbanel,[148] the Malbim,[149] and Rav Moshe Feinstein,[150]

---

146. For more specifics, see *Shulchan Aruch, Even HaEzer* 70:5 and 80:4-10; *Mishneh Torah, Hilchos Ishos* 21:3-7

147. The verse in the *Chumash* speaks of the woman as being an *ezer kenegdo,* or helpmate. The Abarbanel discusses how this helpmate takes care of household needs (Abarbanel on *Bereishis* 95). The Maharal says also that it is a woman's job to take care of household needs. He says that this is evident in *Pirkei Avos* (1:8) which talks about items in the house and then immediately afterwards talks about wives. He says that the sequence shows that wives take care of the home (*Derech Chaim* 1:8). See also *Kesubos* 59b, which outlines these responsibilities.

148. Abarbanel, *Bereishis* 95 (Rav Don Yitzchok Abarbanel, b. 15th century).

149. Malbim on *Bereishis* 2:18 (Rav Maer L. Malbim, b. 19th century).

150. *Igeres Moshe, Orach Chaim* IV, 49.

this assigned role to women fits well with their God-given natures.

The *Malmid HaTalmidim* explains that the exemption of women from positive time-bound commandments works also to help a woman to fulfill her other primary role as wife. As the invaluable and precious helpmate to her husband, a woman could not easily assist him in their important work and attend to the positive time-bound commandments.[151] For example, how could she simultaneously work to eliminate distractions to his Torah learning while she travels about town in search of an *esrog*.

It may be useful to divert momentarily from the subject at hand to discuss this matter of the husband's Torah learning. The learning of Torah is considered the highest possible endeavor for a Jew and the source of greatest divine reward.[152] Learning in this regard does not refer only to study of law in its practical application. It refers also to study as an intellectual enterprise. Learning as such is incumbent only on men.[153] As for women's

---

151. *Malmid HaTalmidim, Parshas Lech Lecha* (Rav Yaakov Anatoli, 13th century); *Malmid HaTalmidim* is also brought by *Kol Bo, Hilchos Milah* 63 and *Halichos Baisa, Pesach HaBayis* 16.

152. Chofetz Chaim, *Ahavos Chesed* 3:4; *Sefer Chofetz Chaim, Pesicha, Asien* 12. See also *Pirkei Avos* 6:6 and *Megillah* 15b.

153. *Kiddushin* 34a; *Berachos* 17a; *Mishneh Torah, Hilchos Talmud Torah* 1:13. See also Rav Moshe Sternbuch, *Moadim U'Zmanim*, vol. I, *siman* 2. He argues that a woman does not receive the reward of a *mitzvah keyumes* for *Limud Torah*, but rather she receives the lesser reward of the general desire to do a mitzvah. The greatest reward results from fullfilling an obligation. A lesser reward is generated from doing an act which is not commanded, per se, but when performed constitutes the fulfillment of a commandment. An example of the latter type is tzitzis. A man is not obligated in the sense of *taryag* mitzvahs to wear fringes.

learning, scholarly opinions vary on which materials and occasions are ideal or appropriate. Let it be mentioned only that many great Jewish leaders have expressed the imperative of women's study of particular parts of Torah under certain circumstances.[154] The subject, which has been much discussed in recent years, is not within the scope of this book. The point for now is that the commandment of *Limud Torah*, or study for its own sake, is incumbent only on men. Since divine reward is greatest for commanded acts,[155] one may wonder what a woman can do to earn divine rewards as significant as a man's reward for *Limud Torah*. The Talmud says the following:

> How do women merit reward? By taking their children to the classroom, by helping their husbands to the house of the Rabbis, and by waiting for their husbands

---

However, he is obligated to wear fringes on four corned garments. By putting on a four corned garment with fringes, a man is fulfilling a mitzvah which is not necessarily always incumbent on him. This is a *mitzvah keyumes*. According to Rav Sternbuch, *Limud Torah* for women is neither an obligation nor a *mitzvah kiumes* (Rav Moshe Sternbuch, contemporary).

154. Chofetz Chaim, *Likutei Halachos* on *Sotah* 21; *Sefer Chasidim* 313; Rav Hirsch says the following: "No less should Israel's daughters learn the content of the Written Law and the duties which they have to perform in their lifetime as daughter and young woman, as mother and housewife. Many times have Israel's daughters saved the purity of the Jewish life and spirit" (Rav Samson Raphael Hirsch, *Horeb* (New York: Soncino Press, 1981), 494, trans. by Dayan Isidor Grunfeld). *Torah Temimah* discusses possible distinctions in choice of material for exceptionally intellectually inclined women (*Torah Temimah, Devarim* 11:48).

155. *Baba Kama* 38a.

until they return from the house of the Rabbis.[156]

In helping her husband to go about his Torah learning, a wife earns for herself the greatest possible divine reward, equal to and sometimes greater than that of her husband.[157] She also benefits her family and society in the highest possible way.[158] Her commitment to his learning, really their learning, is part of the divine plan of team effort.

One may wonder how a woman can receive reward equal to that of her husband for his *Limud Torah*. As mentioned, the Gemara says, "Greater is the one who is commanded and does than the one who is not commanded and does."[159] However, the *Igeres Shmuel* points out that another principle must be taken into consideration as well. The Gemara in *Baba Basra* says, "Greater is the one who enables an act than the one who performs the act."[160] According to the *Igeres Shmuel*, the simultaneous operation of these two principles explain how a husband and wife receive equal reward for the husband's Torah study, and how the wife may even come to merit greater reward.[161]

The dedication of Jewish women to their husband's Torah learning and the acknowledgment of that contribution has been

---

156. *Berachos* 17a; Maharal, *Derosh al HaTorah*, d'h *Shuv omar cah tomar*, in *Cisvei Maharal* (New York: Yodika Prasam, 1966), vol. II, p. 27; Rav Yosef Avraham Wolfe, *Takufa U'Baiyoseha* (B'nei Brak: Nezach), p. 279.

157. *Derosh al HaTorah*, d'h *Shuv omar cah tomar*; *Orach HaShulchan, Yoreh Deiah* 146:20.

158. *Derech Hashem* 1:4:9.

159. *Baba Kama* 38a.

160. *Baba Basra* 9a.

161. *Igeres Shmuel*, (near the end) d'h *VeChain b'inyan hanashim*, in the volume with *Sepharim Kedoshim MeTalmidei Bescht al Sefiras Omer.*, Vol. II (Brooklyn: Bais Hillel, 5753), p. 67.

well demonstrated throughout our history. Rachel, the wife of Rabbi Akiva, relinquished fabulous wealth to marry her husband when he was still an unlearned man. She then lived apart from him for twenty-four years while he pursued his studies in a distant city. When Rabbi Akiva finally returned home, he was escorted by his thousands of devoted pupils. He told them all how his wife shares equally in all they accomplished together.[162]

The book *For Love of Torah* details many more such stories, including that of the Chofetz Chaim and his wife Freida. When they married, the Chofetz Chaim was already well known for his scholarship, and many wealthy families sought to marry him to their daughters and support him in learning. But the Chofetz Chaim married Freida, whose family could offer little support. Many years later, the Chofetz Chaim reflected on the indispensability of Frieda's contribution to his Torah learning. He said: "It is to my wife's credit that I have been able to study Torah all my life and write *sefarim*. She was always happy with her lot and never pursued the enticements of this world. Thanks to her, I was always able to study amid tranquillity."[163]

An especially moving story is that of Chana Perl, the wife of Rav Aaron Kotler. Her story is told as follows:

> The great prince of Torah, R' Aharon Kotler, merited a partner in life whose own appreciation of Torah was a lesson to all. *Rebbetzin* Chana Perl's understanding of the Torah's inestimable worth and the respect she accorded its students was a lesson from which the students themselves had much to learn. She would often ask rhetorically, "Who am I compared to a ben Torah?" She would rise in respect for any student of Torah —

162. *Kesubos* 63a.
163. Rabbi Shimon Finkelman, *For Love of Torah* (Brooklyn: Mesorah Publications, 1992), p. 143.

even a young child.

She forever prayed, and even fasted, for the continued flourishing of her husband's yeshivah and success of its individual students....

She once remarked that she could not recall ever having willfully distracted her husband from his learning. On another occasion, she revealed that all her married life she had prayed that if a Heavenly decree involving R' Aharon's health were to be issued, it should be executed upon her instead.

Such was not to be. On 3 Kislev, 5721, R' Aharon lay hospitalized as his end drew near. The *rebbetzin* stood by his bedside and wept. *"Es vet zein gut* (It will be good),"* she managed to say. *"Es is shoin gut* (It is already good),"* he comforted her.

In R' Aharon's final moments, *Rebbetzin* Chana Perl withdrew to the doorway of the room, so that his closest disciples who drank thirstily from his wellspring of Torah could surround him as he returned his soul to his Maker.[164]

As with many of the points of this book, these stories demonstrate elevated levels of behavior whose attainment and even whose meaning may evade us. Nevertheless, the righteous devotion and sense of inner accomplishment of these heroic people should ring true to our hearts and should inspire us in the differing invaluable contributions of men and women to Torah.

Returning to the original discussion on the exemption of

---

164. *For Love of Torah*, pp. 144-145.

women from positive time-bound commandments, in the views of the *Malmid HaTalmidim* and the Abudraham, domestic peace could be jeopardized by the obligation of both men and women in time-bound commandments. What if a husband needed his wife's assistance in some important matter as the time for *Krias Shema* comes and goes. Does she attend to her husband as required or to the commandment of *Krias Shema*? One way or another, some marital discord could arise in such a situation even amongst well-meaning people. Says the Abudraham: "We find that the Great Name written in holiness and purity is erased in water in order to make peace between man and woman."[165] He is referring to the making of the *Sotah* waters, which test for marital infidelity.[166] These waters are made by mixing water with the letters of Hashem's name which have been scratched off a parchment. While ordinarily requiring extreme care in the treatment of Hashem's name, the Torah allows for this unusual treatment since it may serve to promote domestic peace.

The reader may wonder why, given the above explanations, that unmarried women are also exempt from positive time-bound commandments. After all, the reasons given by the Abudraham and the *Malmid HaTalmidim* concern the marital relationship. The reader may ask the following: if household duties are the reason for the exemption, then why are women without household duties also exempted?

A number of *Acharonim* address this question.[167] Perhaps

---

165. *Sefer Abudraham, Seder Tefillas shel Chol, Birchas HaMitzvos U'Mishpatim.*

166. *Bamidbar* 5:23.

167. For a list, see *Halichos Baisa, Kuntris Pasach HaBayis*, section 16. It is intersting to note that none of the many sources brought in the list in *Halichos Baisah* propose that perhaps women should be obligated in those commandments. The exemption from the

the most concise answer offered is that unmarried women are also exempted in order to limit eliminate a possible deterrent to their getting married. An unmarried woman, despite her natural desire to be married,[168] might be otherwise reluctant to shed her obligation in the positive time-bound commandments. The Torah exempts unmarried women for the promotion of marriage.[169] Of course, the value placed by Torah on marriage is immeasurable. As the Chumash says, "Be fruitful and multiply"[170] and "It is not good for man to be alone."[171] The Talmud says, "The world was created for fruition and increase as it is said, 'Not for desolation did He create it. He formed it to be inhabited,' "[172] [173] and "Hashem favors procreation over [the construction of] the Holy Temple."[174] The Talmud says also, "All who are not involved in fruition and increase are as though they shed blood, as the verse, 'The man who sheds a man's blood, by a man shall his blood be shed,'[175] is followed by 'Be

---

Gemara is clear. Additionally, none of the sources suggest that the exemption is due to any elevated spiritual status of women over men, an increasingly popular but apparently incorrect notion which shall be discussed at some length later on in this book.

168. *Yevamos* 113a and 118b.

169. Rav Shlomo Aaron Wertheimer, *Divrei Shlomo* (beginning), found in the back of *Abudraham HaShalaim*, (Jerusalem: 5723), p. 405. (Rav Wertheimer was a *dayan* in Jerusalem in the middle of this century.) See also *Tziunim L'Torah, Clal* 39 who says that marriage is so much a woman's purpose in life that there is no point in giving extra commandments to an unmarried woman.

170. *Bereishis* 1:28.

171. *Bereishis* 2:18.

172. *Yesheyahu* 45:18.

173. *Eduyos* 1:13.

174. *Talmud Yerushalmi, Kesuvos* 5:7.

175. *Bereishis* 9:6.

fruitful and multiply.' "[176] [177] The Talmud says also, "The man without a wife dwells with no happiness, no blessing, and no good."[178] The Midrash says, "A woman does not find rest except in the home of her husband"[179] and "A woman's yearning is only for her husband."[180] The Midrash says also, "Adam refers to the union of male and female."[181] The *Tziunim L'Torah* says that marriage is a woman's primary purpose in life.[182] In the words of Rav Hirsch, "The Jewish Sages know nothing holier or nearer to God than marriage...."[183] At the wedding celebration we thank Hashem for creating "joy and gladness, groom and bride, mirth, song, pleasure, delight, love, brotherhood, peace, and companionship."[184] Such is the importance of marriage that even some commandments may be pushed off to protect it.

Another approach to the question of why, according to the Abudraham's reason, unmarried women are also exempted is to consider the general philosophy behind ascribing reasons for commandments. The *Sefer HaChinuch*, a *Rishon* from the four-teenth century, comprised a list of the 613 commandments and an elaboration of their reasons and meanings. He was a strong proponent of finding human understandings of reasons for the commandments. In explaining the Talmud's reason for the seven day waiting period of a woman in *niddah*, he says the following:

---

176. *Bereishis* 9:7.
177. *Yevamos* 63b.
178. *Yevamos* 62b. See Maharal, *Chidushei Agados* for an explanation of this *Chazal*.
179. *Rus Rabbah* 2:15.
180. *Midrash Rabbah, Bereishis* 20:7.
181. *Zohar, Nasso*, 145b. See also *Talmud Yerushalmi, Berachos* 9:1.
182. *Tziunim L'Torah, Clal* 39 (Rav Yosef Engel).
183. *Judaism Eternal*, vol. II, p. 90.
184. *Sidur, Sheva Berachos, sixth blessing*.

> In truth, this reason does not comprise the Rabbi's
> entire knowledge of the intentions on the matter. It is
> only to give some sense of it. Commandments carry
> many meanings and reasons aside from the central
> ones.[185]

The seven day waiting period for a woman in *niddah*, like the
exemption of woman from positive time-bound commandments,
is incumbent on all women. This includes even those women
whose inclusion is not explained by the general reason for the
commandment.[186] According to the *Sefer HaChinuch*, the reasons offered by the Rabbis are oftentimes meant to show us particular benefits of a commandment and not meant to give the
complete explanation. As said previously, Hashem's commandments contain myriad meanings, some of which are understandable to people and some of which transcend our ability to understand. In other words, the ultimate reasons are beyond us and
some of the benefits are understandable to us. The part to which
we are privy cannot explain the whole commandment, but the
Rabbis offer these partial reasons to enhance our appreciation of
the commandment.

The *Kasav Sofer* appears to apply this idea directly to the
matter of the exemption of women from positive time-bound
commandments. In his explanation of the view of the *Kol Bo*,
who also says that women are exempt because of the demands
of household duties, the *Kasav Sofer* says the following:

> We must say that the reason given is not meant to
> explain everything. Rather, it is to give some logic to
> the matter of why women are not obligated in these
> commandments. He did not say it to give the precise

---

185. *Sefer HaChinuch, Parshas Terumah, Mitzvah* 95.
186. Relevant cases are beyond our scope of discussion.

halachic reasons.[187]

The *Kasav Sofer* says also that the reason of household duties is sometimes used as the operative factor in granting exemptions in similar matters which are decided on a rabbinical level.[188] However, the reason of household duties as an explanation of the Torah's exemption is not meant to explain the exemption for all cases.

In a similar manner, the *Chemdas Yisrael* says that the Talmud's legal ruling of *lo darshinan tama d'kra*,[189] or "not applying the reasons of the verse," makes unnecessary any specific halachic explanation of the exemption. This is a reference to the Talmud's decision not to use reasons for Torah commandments to render legal decisions. In view of this, a halachic explanation of the exemption from positive commandments is unnecessary.[190] In other words, the Abudraham was not attempting to explain the Torah's halachic rationale behind the exemption, for such an explanation would be halachically inapplicable. Rather, the Abudraham offered a general explanation of the benefits of the exemption.

Another approach to the question of why, given the reason of household duties, unmarried women are also exempt from positive time-bound commandments is that of the *Pardeis Yosef.* He raises the question and answers as follows:

---

187. *Kasav Sofer, She'elos U'Tshuvos, Orach Chaim, Tshuvah* 75, *d'h L'mayshivas* (Rav Avraham Shmuel Binyamin Sofer, b. 19th century).

188. *Kasav Sofer, She'elos U'Tshuvos, Orach Chaim, Tshuvos* 53 and 75.

189. *Baba Matzia* 115a.

190. *Chemdas Yisrael, Nair Mitzvos,* near the beginning, *d'h HaAcharonim,* as published in Pietrokow, vol. I, p.37 (Rav Maer Don Palatski, b. 19th century).

> The intention is that since women have a duty to their husbands, the Holy Torah exempted them and, in not differentiating [*lo plug*] from the case of unmarried women, exempted unmarried women too.[191]

Thus, the law applies to all people, even though its revealed benefits are not relevant to all individuals. This is a common device in Talmudic thought as shall be explained.

The halachic device of *lo plug* or "undifferentiated" is typically employed by the Rabbis to prevent confusion about the parameters of a ruling. For example, reading with illumination from Shabbos candles is prohibited for fear that the reader may inadvertently tip the lamp to increase the light. Such a mistake could be made by a well-meaning person who is engrossed in his book. The prohibition of reading by candlelight on Shabbos applies even if the candle is out of reach of the reader. For example, the candle could be mounted high on a wall. By prohibiting all reading by candlelight, the Rabbis prevent confusion over questions which could otherwise arise in the determination of which heights are permissible.[192] The same type of legal device is employed in the secular world regarding traffic lights. Drivers must stop at red lights regardless of whether other cars are on the road. At three in the morning at a red light on an empty country road, a driver must stop the car and wait until the light turns green. This inclusion of all drivers to the rule of stopping at red lights prevents a loosening of observance of the rule when it is needed.

The *Pardeis Yosef* seems to say that the logic of *lo plug* is operating in the written Torah's exemption of women from posi-

---

191. *Pardeis Yosef, Bereishis* 2:2, *d'h VeYaish l'heyaire* (Rav Yosef Patsanovski, b. 19th century).
192. *Shabbos* 12b and 149a.

tive time-bound commandments.[193] Naturally, on a written Torah level, the device of *lo plug* is not the operative factor in the law since Torah laws are based on a multitude of reasons, many of which transcend human logic. Rather, *lo plug* on a written Torah level serves to give us some sense of the practical implications of the commandment. In our case, the ruling is given for married women who comprise the majority of cases. Unmarried women are included in the exemption even though the operative reason does not apply to them.

As an added note by the author on the last point, it may help to understand that until recently the average age of marriage for Jewish women was in the teenage years. While the age of marriage for a person must be decided on a case to case basis, the Talmud expresses clearly that the ideal age for males and females is quite young.[194] The Mishnah says, "At eighteen [the child should be brought] to the wedding canopy."[195] The Gemara says, "Until [a man] reaches twenty years of age, the

---

193. The *poskim* disagree as to whether the reason of *lo plug* can be given with regard to commandments. The Shach (*Yoreh Deah* 86:8) says they may be so used and the *Crasi U'Plasi* (*Yoreh Deah* 86:4) says they may not be so used (*Olas Nidava* [Edison, NJ: 1982] p.133). The *Sha'agas Aryeh* explains *lo plug* as the reason why women are not obligated to perform *Bris Milah* (*Sha'agas Aryeh, She'elos U'Tshuvos* 53). The Maharsham brings a proof that Tosfos holds *lo plug* may be used with regard to commandments (Marasham, *She'elos U'Tshuvos* 3:88).

194. The *Talmud, Sanhedrin* 76b, suggests marrying sons and daughters as they reach puberty. See also *Kiddushin* 29b-30a; *Talmud Yerushalmi, Kesuvos* 68-69. The *Shulchan Aruch* says that a man should be married by age 18 (*Shulchan Aruch, Even HaEzer* 1). Again, people of our generation should consult with a Rav in order to handle the matter properly.

195. *Pirkei Avos* 5:21.

Holy One, blessed be He, sits and waits [and asks] 'When will he be married?' When he reaches the age of twenty and is still unmarried, [the Holy one] says, 'Blasted be his bones.' "[196] The Gemara says as well, "The one who loves his wife as himself and honors her more than himself, who leads his sons and daughters on the straight path, and marries them near the time of their puberty, on him the verse says, 'And you shall know that peace shall be in your tents and you will not sin.' "[197] The Chofetz Chaim says, "It is a commandment of the Sages to marry off one's sons and daughters close to their age of maturity."[198] The Shelah HaKodesh says many generations ago the courts would compel marriage on people who were unmarried past the age of twenty.[199] Throughout Jewish history, women were married young, and prior to that marriage were probably engaged in the kind of household activities which fall typically on married women. Our emotional involvement with the question of why unmarried women are exempt from positive time-bound commandments may be very much a product of our era and its social dilemmas. In previous centuries, the question was not such an issue in part because there were not in practicality so many individuals who stood as exceptions to the Abudraham's explanation.

It should be noted also that in addition to the Abudraham

---

196. *Kiddushin* 29b.
197. *Sanhedrin* 76b. Other Gemaras give a slightly broader age range for sons in special circumstances, but never past the early twenties (*Kiddushin* 29b-30a).
198. *Chofetz Chaim, Sefer HaMitzvos HaKatzar, M'A* 110.
199. Shelah HaKodesh, *Shnei Luchos HaBris* 100 as brought by *Meam Loez, Bereishis* 1:28. It would seem, however, that the man and the woman could not be forced into a specific marriage without their ultimate consent (*Kiddushin* 1b).

and the *Malmid HaTalmidim*, there are a number of other Rishonim who give the reason of household duties as the reason for the exemption. In particular, there is the Ritva,[200] the *Tosfos HaRid*,[201] the Rashbatz,[202] and the Rabbeinu Manoach.[203]

200. Ritva (Rav Yom Tov ibn Asevilli, b. 14th century) is brought by *Torah Temimah*, *Shemos* 13:9.
201. *Tosfos HaRid* (Rav Yeshayah of Trani HaZaken, b. 12th century) is brought by *Torah Temimah*, *Shemos* 13:9.
202. Rashbatz, *Magen Avos* 2:6 (Rav Shimon Duran, b. 14th century). Brought by *Olas Nidavah*, p.132.
203. Rabbeinu Manoach, *Sefer Menuchah* 7:8 (13th century).

Eight

The Exemption According to Acharonim: The Maharal

    While the Rishonim brought in the last chapter offer practical reasons for the exemption of women from positive time-bound commandments, the Maharal offers a philosophical explanation which seems to stem from his general portrayal of the spiritual natures of men and women. Accordingly, this chapter discusses the larger topic of the spiritual attributes of each gender as discussed by the Maharal. This chapter will attempt to show as well how the Maharal's explanation of the exemption and the spiritual natures of men and women can fit into a larger understanding of Jewish life and Torah centered living.

    The Maharal's explanation of the exemption combines his depiction of the distinct spiritual natures of each gender and the distinct function of the two groups of commandments called positive and negative commandments. Positive commandments such as Tefillin give structure and direction to the world. Negative commandments such as the prohibition against stealing prevent us from damaging the world. Simultaneously, men are compared to the philosophical quality of *tzurah* or that which lends form and direction to the physical. Men are obligated in

the positive time-bound commandments because of their possession of this positive spiritual quality. Men and women are equally obligated in the negative commandments because both gen-
ders are capable of destructive acts which harm the world.[204]

This analysis contradicts a popular misconception that the
Maharal views men as being obligated in the positive time-
bound commandments because men are less spiritual than are
women and need the commandments to spiritualize them. There
are a number of serious logical flaws with such an argument,
including the peculiar assumption that commandments exist
strictly to spiritualize insufficiently spiritual beings. This issue
shall be discussed in more detail in chapter twelve of this book.
Moreover, the Maharal's writings contain numerous essays
where he attributes predominant and higher spirituality to the
masculine nature.[205]

The misconception of the Maharal's view on the exemption
of women from positive time-bound commandments may stem
from a misreading of his discussion of the soft language used to
address the women at the receiving of Torah at Mt. Sinai. The
Maharal explains that the women were spoken to as such to let
them know of the tremendous reward designated to them for
their support of their husband's Torah learning. Since Torah
learning is incumbent only on men, the women might not see
how they can gain reward from it. Accordingly, the women
might try to prevent their husbands from receiving the Torah.
The women were spoken to first and in soft language to let them
know that their equal and possibly superior share in the reward

---

204. Maharal, *Tiferes Yisrael* 4.
205. Maharal, *Derech Chaim* 2:9 (on the *Mishnah: Amar lehem tzoo
    u'rahoo*) *d'h' U'mizeh*; *Chidushei Agados, Makos*, 23b, *d'h
    U'mayatah*; *Derech Chaim* 1:5 (on the *Mishnah: Al tarbeh
    sichah im haishah*) *d'h Aval da*; *Tiferes Yisrael* 4 and 28; *Nasivos
    Olam, Hakdamah* (towards the end).

for Torah learning comes through their assistance of their husband's and children's learning.[206]

Furthermore, harsher language is used towards the men to show that men toil in Torah in part to develop their strong and active natures in a proper fashion. Women, by nature, are more tranquil. Rigorous involvement in continuous Torah study would not be relevant to such personalities.[207]

The Maharal says also that this tranquillity of women bears some parallel to the tranquillity of the world to come. Accordingly, a woman's reward for supporting her family's Torah learning is more readily transferred from this world to the next. The feminine personality is more readied for the receiving of reward.[208] As a note, this does not mean that women receive more reward for the same work.[209] The Mishnah says, "According to the work is the reward."[210] A commentator on the Maharal says, "The woman earns her place in the next world

---

206. Maharal, *Derosh al HaTorah*, middle, *d'h Shuv omar cah tomar (in Sifrei Maharal, p. 27)*.

207. *Derosh al HaTorah, d'h Shuv omar cah tomar*.

208. *Derosh al HaTorah, d'h Shuv omar cah tomar*.

209. The Maharsha says that a man, by virtue of his having extra commandments, will merit more reward than a woman who fulfills her commandments at a level equivalent to the man. This is logical as he has done more work. The Maharsha says as well that a man may receive more punishment (*Agados Maharsha, Menachos* 43b). However, for the commandments that are required of a woman the Talmud says the following: "According to the verse, 'When a man or woman commit any sin' (*Bamidbar* 5:6). Scripture thus makes a woman equal to a man with regard to all punishments prescribed in the Torah" (*Kiddushin* 35a). Of course, a woman may dedicate herself without limit to her commandments and earn for herself the greatest possible reward.

210. *Pirkei Avos* 5:23.

just like a man. There is no difference whatsoever."[211] The Maharal, in his comments on the transferability of reward to the next world, is discussing dynamics of the soul and the workings of divine reward. These are lofty matters which are not especially relevant to everyday life. Naturally, these matters are easily misunderstood when one tries to think of them in mundane terms.

One may observe that the Maharal's discussion of male activity and female tranquillity makes no explicit reference to spirituality. His discussion concerns only the active and aggressive masculine nature and the more tranquil female nature. The more active masculine nature suits well with study of the Torah. The more tranquil feminine nature, as said, bears some parallel to the world to come as that world is a place for receiving reward. This tranquillity is a precious type of spirituality but it is not the only type of spirituality. Moreover, the discussion does not mention the positive time-bound commandments. It refers only to *Limud Torah* which is not a positive time-bound commandment.[212]

The author should point out that these discussions of general propensities refer largely to the natures within individuals. Whether or not a person develops himself or herself is a different matter. In our generation, this gap between human potential and reality is seriously widened. Our sins and the influence of the atrophying cultures around us divorces us even more from our true selves.

Furthermore, these generalities do not speak for every person within a gender but for most people within a gender. As the Rambam says, "Whatever the law teaches, whether it be of an

---

211. *Perakim BiMishnaso shel Maharal MePrague* (Tel Aviv: Yad Mordechi, 1983), pp. 324-325.
212. See *Tosefta, Kiddushin* 1:10.

intellectual, a moral, or a practical character, is founded on that which is the rule and not on that which is the exception."[213] There are naturally tranquil men and naturally active women. One must remember also that the personality descriptions appear here in translation from the Hebrew. The words "activity" and "tranquillity" are not precisely equivalent terms for the language of the Maharal.

The connection between spiritual nature and religious responsibility of each gender is seen elsewhere in the Maharal's writings.[214] In *Derech Chaim*, the Maharal details the numerous components of the soul. Some of these components have leanings toward more purely spiritual matters and others toward more physical matters of Torah life. The Maharal says that the masculine nature has more of the exclusively spiritually inclined components and these correspond to the man's religious activities.

> And because the feminine leans towards the physical, her completion does not reside with the distinctly spiritual matters. Certainly she has these [purely spiritual traits] but not as much.[215]

What the Maharal seems to be outlining here are the differing spiritual orientations of the masculine and the feminine natures. Since his discussion concerns the attributes of the soul, he is out-

---

213. *Moreh Nevuchim* 3:34, translation by M. Friedlander from *The Guide for the Perplexed* (New York: Dover Publications, 1956), p. 328.

214. *Derech Chaim* 2:9 (on the *Mishnah: Amar lehem tzoo u'rahoo*) *d'h' U'mizeh; Chidushei Agados, Makos*, 23b, *d'h U'mayatah; Derech Chaim* 1:5 (on the *Mishnah: Al tarbeh sichah im haishah*) *d'h Aval da; Tiferes Yisrael* 4 and 28.

215. *Derech Chaim* 2:9 (on the *Mishnah: Amar lehem tzoo u'rahoo*) *d'h' U'mizeh.*

lining particular manifestations of spirituality. Both the masculine and the feminine personalities are spiritual. However, the spirituality of the feminine leans more towards the practical concerns of religious life. These practical concerns, such as running a Jewish household, require religious faith, wisdom, ingenuity, sensitivity, creativity and dedication. Note, for example, the Talmudic discussion of a woman's ability to make guests feel comfortable and to perform acts of lovingkindness.[216] These are the qualities of a *b'tzelem Elokim*,[217] a person created in Hashem's image. As Shlomo HaMelech said about an ideal Jewish woman: "A woman who fears the Lord, she shall be praised,"[218] "She opened her mouth with wisdom,"[219] and "She looked constantly to the ways of her house."[220] Rav Hirsch, in his tireless efforts to translate these ideas for his confused era, describes this woman as "the quiet and wise counselor of her husband for the welfare of the community."[221] He said also "by word and deed she teaches self-sacrifice and love."[222] Without question, her role in Jewish life is multifaceted and rich, and so too are the spiritual qualities given to her to carry out this role.

Indeed, both men and women carry within awesome spiritual potentials. Both men and women are precious to Hashem and

---

216. *Halichos Bas Yisrael* 1:15.
217. Chofetz Chaim, *Ahavos Chesed* 2:2. The Chofetz Chaim describes *b'tzelem Elokim* as the ability to emulate Hashem's characteristics such as *chesed*; Rambam in *Moreh Nevuchim* describes *b'tzelm Elokim* as referring to the possession of intellect (Malbim on *Bereishis* 1:26). The Malbim describes it as freedom to act in a moral or immoral fashion (Malbim on *Bereishis* 1:26).
218. *Mishlei* 31:30.
219. *Mishlei* 31:26.
220. *Mishlei* 31:27.
221. *Judaism Eternal*, vol. II, p.89.
222. *Judaism Eternal*, vol. II, p.89.

are created in Hashem's image. Furthermore, being created in Hashem's image means creativity, compassion, generosity, and intellect as well as myriad other qualities. But, as has been discussed, since men and women were created to express different aspects of spiritual qualities, it would not be fitting for both to bear identical spiritual natures. Man is the more active and direct agent of world transformation to Torah values.[223] Woman is the invaluable and precious helpmate to man in this endeavor.[224] (Remember the point from chapter four about all Jews being ultimately helpers in Hashem's mission). The man is better equipped to handle some areas of religious life and the woman is better equipped to handle others. The woman's religious role tends to include more practical activities (which is not to exclude her many predominately emotional and intellectual activities) and, according to the Maharal, the woman's spiritual nature is designed to enable her to excel at that vital role. Hers is a religious function, a divinely ordained and designed activity.

In a very real sense, it works much like the role of all Jews. We are partially spiritual and partially physical beings.[225] We do spiritual work within the physical world.[226] As the Ramchal says:

> However, the deep design of the Blessed One's wisdom was to order things so that even though man is by necessity immersed in the physical, as we have written, he should be able to attain spiritual completion and to be elevated to purity and loftiness through the physical itself and the activities of the body....And this is

---

223. Maharasha on *Baba Basra* 117a, *d'h Kol mi sh'aino*; *Judaism Eternal*, vol. II, p. 51.
224. *Judaism Eternal*, vol. II, pp. 51-52.
225. Malbim on *Bereishis* 2:18; *Meom Loez, Bereishis* 1:26, *Bereishis* 1:27 and *Bereishis* 2:7.
226. *Derech Hashem* 1:4:4.

because the Creator, may His name be blessed, gave man boundaries and rules to use in his interaction with the world and with the creations [of Hashem] so that [they are used] as they were intended. When man makes use of the them according to the boundaries, rules, and intentions that the Creator, may His name be blessed, commanded, then the physical work and the physical matter itself become acts of spiritual completion. And through this a person can bring within himself completion and tremendous elevation.[227]

Accordingly, every commandment has physical parameters in order to engage our physicality.[228] One gender in general may sometimes undertake more conspicuoulsy spiritual activities, but these have a distinct physical aspect to them. Even the learning of Torah, the highest of activities, is done with eyes, mouths, hands, and books. The Torah student spends a surprising amount of time flipping pages. Even at its purest moments, Torah study is done with words which are devices by which physical beings relate to abstractions. We all have conspicuously physical aspects to our lives. These physical aspects are essential because our job is to bring spirituality to the physical world.[229] Rav Hirsch explains this as follows: "The Word of God knows no division of life into two compartments, the so-called religious, directed to God, and the other, the profane, which has nothing to do with divine matters. God takes the whole of life for His service, demands it for the calling of "Adam", and in the very first place, the family and civil life.[230]

The Torah dedicates considerable discussion to the emo-

---

227. *Derech Hashem* 1:4:4.
228. *Derech Hashem* 1:4:5 and 4:5:2.
229. *Derech Hashem* 1:4:7.
230. Rav Hirsch on *Bereishis* 1:28.

tional and intellectual responsibilities of the Jewish woman. After all, the rich emotional life within each woman is crucial to the progress of the Jewish nation. Her potential to bring warmth and understanding to the practical matters of running a household have already been mentioned. Besides this is the enthusiasm and generosity that Jewish women have demonstrated in the overall national mission. The Chumash tells us of the "generous heart" of the women of Moshe's generation who played such a crucial role in the building of the Mishkan.[231] Indeed, the emotional component to Judaism is fundamental. The Chumash tells us "you shall love the Lord your God with all your heart."[232] The Gemara says that "the Holy One, Blessed be He, wants the heart."[233] The punishments detailed in *Devarim* came about because "you have not served Hashem your Lord with a good heart."[234] The commandment of prayer, which is considered one of the world's three pillars,[235] is derived in part from the verse "and to serve Him with all your heart."[236] Prayer is considered "service of the heart."[237] David HaMelech told his son,

---

231. *Shemos* 35:22.; Ramban on *Shemos* 38:8; *Chaim shel Osher* (vol. II, p.36) draws a connection between this "generous heart" of the women by the *Mishkan* and the personality trait of lovingkindness. For a discussion in English, see *Fulfillment in Marriage*, vol. II, pp. 30-31. Most of the ideas in this paragraph are drawn from *Chaim shel Osher*, vol. II, chapter 2.
232. *Devarim* 6:5.
233. *Sanhedrin* 106b.
234. *Devarim* 28:47.
235. *Pirkei Avos* 1:2. As for the varying types of obligations in prayer, see *Berachos* 3:2 and 20b; *Mishneh Torah, Hilchos Tefillah* 1:1:1; *Shulchan Aruch, Orach Chaim* 106:1; *Mishnah Berurah* 106:4.
236. *Sefer HaMitzvos HaKatzar, M'A* 7.
237. *Sefer HaMitzvos HaKatzar, M'A* 7.

"Solomon, my son, know the God of your father and serve Him with a complete heart."[238]

Given the importance of emotion in divine service, one should not be surprised to hear of the historically close relationship between Jewish women and prayer. Many people relate fond memories of their grandmothers uttering prayers and reading *Tehillim* with sincerity and feeling. Furthermore, the more public contributions of Jewish women throughout history have often been in the realm of prayer. As said earlier, a woman's contribution to Jewish life is done primarily in the private realm of the Jewish home. This is arranged by divine design. More public matters are generally handled by the men; although men's contributions in the private realm of the Jewish home are also essential to Jewish life. Nevertheless, many halachahs concerning prayer are derived from the prayers of Chana.[239] In addition to her contributions through private life (and no doubt because of them) she made this public contribution in the realm of prayer. Interestingly, these fervent prayers of Chana were prayers for Hashem to give her children.[240]

The Torah has much to say also on the woman's intellectual connection to Torah life. The ingenuity and intellectual sensitivity required to run a Jewish home have already been mentioned

---

238. *Divrei HaYamim* 1:28:9.
239. *Berachos* 31a-31b; *Meam Loez* on *Shmuel* 1:1:13 (Rav Shmuel Yerushalmi, contemporary). These include prayer being made inaudible to others but with moving lips, with concentration of the heart on the words, and the prohibition against prayer while one is intoxicated. There are opinions that we learn as well not to add prayers to those codified by the Great Assembly. The extensiveness of Chana's prayers may have lead to a shortening of Shmuel's life (*Meam Loez, Shmuel* 1:1:12).
240. *Shmuel* 1:1:11.

here; although they really cannot be overemphasized. As the verse in *Mishlei* says, "The wisdom of woman builds her home."[241] On this verse, Rav Shlomo Wolbe says: "Women master many areas of wisdom, and building a proper home demands them all."[242] It must be mentioned as well the wisdom of many Jewish women often achieved in many areas of human affairs. Sarah's counsel to Avraham concerning the inappropriateness of keeping Hagar and Ishmael in the house[243] was a pivotal moment in Jewish history. Furthermore, a woman's knowledge of the ethics and practical laws of Torah life go hand in hand with her *Avodas Hashem*. As the *Akeidas Yitzchok* says, " 'From the man this [she] was taken,'[244] and like him she is able to understand and comprehend matters of piety."[245] In the words of Rav Hirsch:

> The fact is that while women are not exposed to specialized Torah study or theoretical knowledge of the Law, which are reserved for the Jewish man, such understanding of our sacred literature as can teach the fear of the Lord and the conscientious fulfillment of our duty, and all such knowledge as is essential to the adequate execution of our tasks should indeed form part of the mental and spiritual training not only of our

241. *Mishlei* 14:1.
242. Rav Shlomo Wolbe, *Kuntris Hadrachah Lekalos*, p. 33 (from *Fulfillment in Marriage*, vol. II, pp. 24-25.) (Rav Shlomo Wolbe, contemporary).
243. *Bereishis* 21:12.
244. *Bereishis* 2:23.
245. *Akeidas Yitzchok* 9:8. As explained earlier, the *Akeidas Yitzchok* says that this intellectual function of woman is contingent on her being a proper helpmate to her husband. See beginning of chapter four.

sons, but of our daughters as well.[246]

Many great scholars have stressed this latter point with regard to the women of recent generations.[247]

In sum to the whole discussion, a Jewish woman applies her spirituality to physical matters of the Torah and to more purely spiritual matters of the Torah. Both are spiritual acts. The feminine personality designed to do all of this is tremendously important to this world. As Rav Shlomo Wolbe says:

> Women must preserve, at all costs, their qualities as women and not exchange them for those of men. If, for example, the family financial situation necessitates a woman's helping with the livelihood, she should not lose sight of her feminine characteristics. Sometimes this is not easy; women are being drawn more and more away from their natural feminine tendencies toward masculine ways of doing things. When this happens, confusion sets in, and the natural marriage relationship becomes undermined. This confusion is one of the reasons for the widespread disruption of the home in modern society.[248]

---

246. Rav Samson Raphael Hirsch, *The Hirsch Siddur* (New York: Feldheim, 1978), p. 122.
247. *Sefer Chasidim* 313 (Jerusalem: Mosad HaRav Kook, 5743); *Chofetz Chaim, Likutei Halachos, Sotah* 21. It should be noted further that the Torah is not out to repress any person's intelligence, Heaven forbid. Women with leanings toward abstract thought have numerous study materials available to develop that interest. A woman's primary responsibility being in the home does not preclude intellectual development; although intellectual development should not displace her primary responsibility.
248. Rav Shlomo Wolbe, *Kuntris Hadrachah Lekalos* as translated by NC. Nahmoud in *Fulfillment in Marriage*, vol. II, p.24.

Femininity in women must be preserved because of its importance to women, to their families, and to the world. If femininity
were not important, then its preservation would not be a high
priority for us. However, the preservation of femininity is imperative to the success of the Torah community.

It should be mentioned also that the emotional lives of
Jewish men are potentially rich and varied and are essential to
the mission of the Jewish people. The *Avos* display considerable
emotion in their lives. Avraham's love and compassion for his
children,[249] Yitzchok's love for Rivka,[250] Yaakov's longing and
attachment to his son Yosef,[251] and Yosef's heart-wrenching
reunion with his brothers[252] are but a few of the displays of
meaningful emotion by men in the Chumash. Additionally, all
Jews are commanded to love[253] and fear Hashem,[254] to love their
family members and their neighbors,[255] to feel compassion for
the needy,[256] to feel joy on sacred occasions,[257] to feel sadness at
times of mourning,[258] and much more as well.

People sometimes make the mistake of exaggerating the
philosophical characterizations of masculinity and femininity,
formulating overly dichotomized understandings of the differences between men and women. Men are then said to lead strictly intellectual lives, and women emotional lives; or men are said

---

249. *Bereishis* 22:1; Rav Hirsch on *Bereishis* 21:12.
250. *Bereishis* 24:67.
251. *Bereishis* 45:26 and 46:29.
252. *Bereishis* 45:1.
253. *Sefer HaMitzvos HaKatzar, M'A* 3.
254. *Sefer HaMitzvos HaKatzar, M'A* 4.
255. *Kiddushin* 41a; *Sefer HaMitzvos HaKatzar, M'A*. 60.
256. *Sefer HaMitzvos HaKatzar, M'A*. 6.
257. *Sefer HaMitzvos HaKatzar, M'A*. 21.
258. *Kitzur Shulchan Aruch* 126 and 215.

to function strictly in the public domain and women in the private. As shown above in the case of men and emotions and as shown earlier in the case of women and intellect, such portrayals are too simplistic. Regarding public and private life, it can be said similarly that the lives of men and women should not be characterized as being exclusively either public or private according to gender. One may note, for example, that Avraham's experience at the binding of Yitzchok[259] and Moshe's numerous encounters with Hashem at Mount Sinai[260] were all performed in private. While a Jewish woman's life tends to operate predominantly in the private domain, one may note that women participated at the receiving of Torah[261] and at some of the national gatherings in Yerushalayim.[262] Naturally, any participation by Jewish women in national gatherings should be conducted with scrupulously modest behavior. As the Midrash says about Hashem's formation of the first woman, "As He created each limb, He said to her, 'Be a modest woman, a modest woman.' "[263] Thus the imperative of modesty for a woman is programmed into her very being. And to avoid creating any intellectual dichotomies of our own, it should be emphasized as well the importance of modesty in men. As the *Kitzur Shulchan Aruch* says, "It is written, 'And to walk humbly with thy God.'[264] Therefore every man needs to be modest in all his ways."[265] And in a further depiction of the overlapping roles of men and women, the *Sefer Chasidim* says, "All that it says in

---

259. *Bereishis* 22:6.
260. For example, *Shemos* 3.
261. *Shemos* 19:3; *Berachos* 17a.
262. *Devarim* 31:2.
263. *Midrash Rabbah, Bereishis* 18:2.
264. *Michah* 6:8.
265. *Kitzur Shulchan Aruch* 3:1.

Shir HaShirim we should be careful about; to not listen to the voice of a woman, and it is the law as well that a woman should not listen to the voice of a man. All that the man must be careful to avoid, the woman should avoid as well."[266]

As with the subject of women and intellect, some young men read the simple portrayals about gender roles and fear that the Torah is prescribing a shutting off of their emotional and private lives. As explained above, emotions and activities in private are a fundamental part of a Torah-observant man's mission in life.

To some extent, women are allowed to develop emotions whose development in men is hindered by the men's public responsibilities. For example, the workplace may force a man to develop a thick skin which is not easy to shed or simply does not leave time for ready enjoyment of the gentler moments of life. Torah study itself often requires an aggressiveness, albeit a healthy one, which may lead one away from the expression of certain types of emotions.[267] Again, this is all part of the team effort of Jewish family life. The men specialize in some areas of life and the women in others. As discussed previously, the object

---

266. *Sefer Chasidim* 614; On the teaching "And [she] should not go out from the doors of the house except for dire need," the *Reishis Chochmah* says, "The woman that goes out sins and causes others to sin. How does she sin? Women have light *daas*. And possibly she will see men in the marketplace and desire them in her heart, and she will come to have improper thoughts. And possibly she will come to an act. And how does [she] cause others to sin? Just as she desires the men, possibly they will desire her" (*Reishis Chochmah, Derech Eretz* 4:3).

267. *Rashi, Kesuvos* 3a discusses how boys are less free to develop intuition because the toil of Torah study drains their energy. On the other hand, girls have more opportunity to develop their intuition. *Sanhedrin* 111b speaks of the "battle of Torah."

is a greater sum accomplishment through division of labor and personality. No one is being shortchanged by the fact that we do not all have the opportunity to experience everything. In a choir, the bass singer focuses on his voice, and the tenor on his. The sounds may differ but both singers have full opportunity to enjoy music itself. And it is a fuller and richer music than each singer would have experienced by himself trying to sing all the parts at separate times — presuming one person could even master them all. T he various intellectual, emotional, and physical aspects of Torah life are like notes to beautiful music. We each contribute to different aspects of the music, yet we enjoy it together.

It should be mentioned also that malignment of the physical realm of life is not a Torah value. The Torah most definitely condemns physical indulgence.[268] Nevertheless, it provides a life design which wondrously combines physical and more purely spiritual activity.[269] The result is the most holy and human path of living.[270] Fasting, celibacy, and poverty are occasional components of Jewish religious life, but they are not the norm. As the Mishnah says, "If there is no flour, there is no Torah."[271] This is not the case with many of the prevalent non-Torah religions which we have encountered in recent centuries.[272]

It is not surprising therefore to see the Talmud's high praise and encouragement of hard work, including simple physical labor. Rav Hirsch expresses this as follows:

> The Talmudic sages held labour in great honour. Their principle was: "Great is work, for it honours him who

---

268. *Derech Hashem* 1:4:7.
269. *Akeidas Yitzchok, Bereishis, shaar* 12.
270. *Mishlei* 3:17.
271. *Pirkei Avos* 3:21.
272. *Judaism Eternal*, vol. II, p. 196.

does it."[273] They said: "Skin a dead animal in the street
to earn your bread, but do not say, 'I am a priest, a
great man, it is not fitting for me.' "[274, 275]

Rav Hirsch says further that "Handicraft, work with one's hands,
was especially esteemed."[276] He notes also numerous other say-
ings of the Rabbis, such as "Love work and do not seek a high
place"[277] and "The God fearing man who lives by the work of
his hands is doubly well off; he is happy in this life and in the
next."[278]

Naturally, this praise of hard work is not an encouragement
to seek wealth. Wealth is not mentioned in these verses. Nor
does this praise of hard work suggest the pushing off of family
development or Torah learning for the sake of a glamorous
career. As with anything in life, one must understand these say-
ings in their proper context and relation to the rest of Torah. The
point in bringing them is to show the richness and breadth of
Torah life and the place of physical activities within that Torah
life. Those of us who by commandment or other necessity are
involved in more physical tasks are also involved with religious
activity. As the Ramchal says at the conclusion to *Path of the
Just*:

Saintliness is attainable by the man who works a trade
out of necessity just as it is for the one in whose mouth
learning never ceases. As it says, "Hashem created
everything for His purpose"[279] and "In all your ways

---

273. *Nedarim* 49b.
274. *Pesachim* 113a.
275. *Judaism Eternal*, vol. II, p. 164.
276. *Judaism Eternal*, vol. II, p. 164.
277. *Judaism Eternal*, vol. II, p. 164.
278. *Judaism Eternal*, vol. II, p. 164.
279. *Mishlei* 16:4.

know Him and He will straighten your paths."[280, 281]

With regard to a *bochur* in yeshiva, the definition of the phrase "out of necessity" in the foregoing quote is best handled with the help of a Rav. But the point should be readily adaptable to our subject. A woman's activity as a wife and mother and her personality designed in accordance with those functions fits well into the divine plan for spiritual accomplishment for all people. As mentioned earlier, the Midrash says that the divine spirit rests upon a person according to his or her actions.[282] If a person is commanded to focus on some more practical aspects of religious life, then that person can express and achieve spiritual dimensions through those more practical activities. The same applies to a man's activity as a learner of Torah, a husband, and a father. A person may be commanded in activities which distract him from the development of every aspect of his personality. However, the activities he is commanded in are all he needs to develop himself in the enduring areas of life. The commandments define religiousness. Our spiritual natures which enable those religious activities are indeed special and wondrous.

---

280. *Mishlei* 3:6.
281. *Mesillas Yisharim* 26.
282. *Seder Eliyahu Rabbah* 9.

Nine

Other Acharonim on the Exemption

There are many ways to view the function of commandments. On one hand they are decrees from Hashem. By adhering
to His decrees for the sole purpose of doing His will, we develop
humility and thereby grow closer to Him.[283] Alternatively, commandments are wise pathways of living. They prescribe moral
and wholesome living.[284] From a more mystical viewpoint, commandments are links to spiritual worlds, each commandment
spiritualizing different parts of us.[285] These different viewpoints
give rise to different questions and explanations on the exemption of women from positive time-bound commandments. With
Hashem's help, this chapter will present writings from several

---

283. *Chovos HaLevavos, Shaar HaChanieah*: 3-6 with *Shaar HaAvodos HaElokim*. See also *Derech Hashem* 1:4:7.
284. *Moreh Nevuchim* 3:26-27; Rav Samson Raphael Hirsch, *The Nineteen Letters, letter eleven*; *Derech Hashem* 1:4:7.
285. *Meam Loez, Bereishis* 1:27; *Igeres Shmuel*, (near the end) *d'h VeAnu*, (in the volume with *Sepharim Kedoshim M'Talmidei Bescht al Sefiras Omer*, vol. II, [Brooklyn: Bais Hillel, 5753] p. 66).

Acharonim on the subject. Again, it is useful to say that the exemption is ultimately a *Chok*,[286] and none of the following explanations can fully explain the exemption. The matter is settled with faith in Hashem and the wisdom of the Torah which oftentimes supersedes logical grasp.

With the recent proliferation of mystical writings and teachings in the English language, people today often seek mystical understandings of commandments. One understanding of the commandments is based on the division of the 613 commandments into groupings of 365 negative commandments and 248 positive commandments. The negative commandments, such as the prohibition against stealing, are said to correspond to the 365 spiritual blood vessels of the human body.[287] The positive commandments, such as the requirement to love one's neighbor, are said to correspond to the 248 spiritual limbs of the body.[288] In mystical thought, the performance of a specific commandment has the effect of giving spiritual energy to its corresponding body part.[289] So the question goes, how do women obtain the spirituality which flows from performance of the positive time-bound commandments?

Actually, one could pose the same question for any Jew since none of us are responsible for all 613 commandments. *Kohanim* perform commandments which even the King of Israel is forbidden to perform. Examples include the daily lifting of ashes from the altar[290] and blessing the nation with the blessing

---

286. *Igeres Moshe, Orach Chaim* IV, 49. See also chapter six.
287. Maharal, *Chidushei Agados, Makos* 23b; *Meam Loez, Bereishis* 1:27.
288. *Makos* 23b; Maharal, *Chidushei Agados, Makos* 23b.
289. *Meam Loez, Bereishis* 1:27.
290. *Vayikra* 6:3; *Sefer HaChinuch* 132.

of the *Kohanim*.[291] Simultaneously, *Kohanim* are forbidden from performing certain commandments such as attending to the dead when a Israel is available for the task.[292] Other commandments are not relevant to *Kohanim*, such as the giving of *terumah* to *Kohanim*.[293] Some commandments are applicable only to the courts.[294] Moreover, many commandments are unavailable to us due to our being in exile without the *Bais Hamikdash*.[295] By the reckoning of the *Sefer HaChinuch*, only 369 commandments of the 613 in the Torah are in force to the entire nation at the present time.[296] The question should be how does any Jew connect to all 613 commandments in the aforementioned mystical fashion?

Additionally, one may ask what happens when the Rabbis decree a *shev v'al taaseh* (translated: sit and don't do) *Shev v'al taaseh* denotes a Talmudic device whereby on   exempted from a positive commandment in order to safeguard a negative commandment. For example, Shofar blowing is not permitted on Shabbos for fear that a person may inadvertently come to carry the Shofar in a public domain.[297] Shofar blowing is, of course, a commandment from the Torah.[298] So too is waving the Lulav[299] which is likewise exempted on Shabbos.[300] If the 613 command-

---

291. The commandment to bless the nation is listed in *Sefer HaMitzvos HaKatzar M'LS* 58. *Halachahs* concerning eligibility to make the blessing are described in *Mishnah Berurah* 128.
292. *Vayikra* 20:14; *Megillah* 3b.
293. *Devarim* 18:4.
294. *Sefer HaMitzvos HaKatzar, M'A* 65-75.
295. *Sefer HaMitzvos HaKatzar, Hakdamah.*
296. *Sefer HaChinuch, HaErus HaMeChaver.*
297. *Succah* 42b-43a.
298. *Bamidbar* 29:1; *Sefer HaMitzvos,* A 7.
299. *Vayikra* 23:40; *Sefer HaMitzvos,* A 169.
300. *Succah* 42b-43a.

ments are a spiritual food for the 613 parts of the body, then again what happens when a positive commandment is pushed off for a negative one?

In addressing this question, the Mabit tells us that the means for connecting to the 613 commandments is through the general acceptance of the yoke of Torah. Since no person is obligated in all 613 commandments, the mystical benefit of the commandments comes to us not through the actual performance of the commandments but through the acceptance of the authority of the commandments. A person must have a willingness to perform any of the 613 commandments if they were for some reason demanded of him. Such an attitude connects a person to all of the commandments, even those which are not asked of him and those which are impossible to perform at any given time.[301]

The Mabit offers another answer that the collective responsibility of Jews for one another connect each person to all the commandments. Each person has a responsibility to prevent his fellow from violating Torah commandments.[302] This general responsibility establishes a channel to commandments which are not obligatory to that person. Commandments which are not incumbent on any person but are obligatory on the Jewish courts are relevant to each Jew through his general respect of the courts.[303]

It should be added that responsibility for correction of others is a delicate and complex subject. The background and sensitivities of people should be guidelines in determining how to approach them. Quite often, people who are new to Torah should

---

301. Mabit, *Kiriyas Sefer, Hakdamah, perek* 7 (found in back of some editions of the *Mishneh Torah, cheilek* 1) (Rav Moshe Trani, b. 16th century).
302. *Vayikra* 19:17; *Sanhedrin* 27b.
303. Mabit, *Kiriyas Sefer, Hakdamah, perek* 7.

not be approached at all.[304] Rav Chaim Mordechai Katz points
out that a person must be aware of his own motivations when
approaching another. Ego satisfaction in being the one who
approached another is obviously not the proper motivation.
Rather, the goal is to have a positive influence on the other person.[305] The Rambam says that a person should speak pleasantly
and softly when admonishing his friend.[306] According to Rav
Chaim Volozhin, a person who is unable to speak in a pleasant
manner is exempt from the obligation of giving reproof.[307] Rav
Dessler points out that insincere admonition is not only ineffective but is highly sinful in itself due to the pain and suffering it
causes others.[308] Moreover, when giving admonition, a person
must be careful not to embarrass his fellow. It is forbidden to
embarrass a person even in private.[309] Public embarrassment of
another person can result in the loss of one's share in the world
to come.[310]

Returning to the subject of the exemption of women from
positive time-bound commandments, the Baal B'nei Yisaschar
explains that the spiritual benefits of the positive time-bound
commandments in particular come to a woman through the performance of those commandments by her husband. The channel

---

304. See *Sefer Chasidim* 413.
305. *Beair Mechokaik*, pp. 257-8 as brought by Rav Zelig Pliskin,
    Consulting the Wise (Brooklyn, NY: Benei Yakov, 1991), pp.
    186-187. Many of the other sources brought in this paragraph are
    from Rav Zelig Pliskin, *Love Your Neighbor* (Jerusalem: Aish
    HaTorah Publications, 1977), pp. 278-295.
306. *Mishneh Torah, Hilchos Deios* 6:7.
307. Rav Chaim Volozhin, *Keren Rosh* 143.
308. *Michtav MeEliyahu* 3:139.
309. *Vayikra* 19:17; *Eruvin* 16b; *Mishneh Torah, Hilchos Deios* 6:8.
310. *Baba Matzia* 59a.

for this flow stems from the inner connection between husband and wife. As the first man and woman were created initially as one being, the inner connection between them endures.[311]

Many Acharonim offer views in accordance with that of the Abudraham and the *Malmid HaTalmidim* that the woman's exemption from the positive time-bound commandments results from the structure of her relationship to her husband. The *Sefer HaChaim Tovim* says that the halachic dynamics of the marriage procedures obligate a woman with marital responsibilities to her husband. Accordingly, she is not in a position to take on the positive time-bound commandments.[312] The *Sefer HaChaim Tovim* adds the following caveat:

> Even though the wife is obligated to her husband, Heaven forbid that he treat her like a maidservant. Rather, he should build her up like an important woman, and furthermore, he is obligated to her according to the conditions of his marriage to her. The Rabbis say that a man should love his wife as himself and honor her more than himself....It appears that they are both important and the two are obligated to each other, until it is difficult to distinguish between them.[313]

In sum, the halachic exemption flows from the halachic features of the marriage procedures. The practical application is that the husband is obligated in the positive time-bound commandments

---

311. Baal B'nei Yisaschar, *Derech Pikudecha, Hakdamah* 9:4 (Rav Tzvi Elimelech Shapiro, b. 18th century).
312. Chaim ben Betzalel , *Sefer HaChaim, sof perek* 5 as brought by *Takufa U'Baiyoseha*, p. 271 (R. Chaim ben Betzalel, older brother of the Maharal, b. 16th century). A similar view is given by *Sefer Chasidim* 611.
313. *Sefer HaChaim, sof perek* 5.

and the wife is not, but both people are obligated to treat one another with respect and consideration.

Rav Hirsch, using a very practical view of commandments, offers another explanation which takes into consideration their symbolic value:

> All positive time-bound commandments are meant, by symbolic procedures, to bring certain facts, principles, ideas, and resolutions, afresh to our minds from time to time to spur us on afresh and to fortify us to realize them to keep them. God's Torah takes it for granted that our women have greater fervour and more faithful enthusiasm for their God serving calling, and that this calling runs less danger in their case than in that of men from the temptations which occur in the course of business and professional life. Accordingly, it does not find it necessary to give women these repeated spurring reminders to remain true to their calling, and warnings against weaknesses in their business lives [314]

In addition to this greater fervour of Jewish women for "their God serving calling," Rav Hirsch in the same passage mentions the trust put on women at the receiving of Torah and the key role played by Jewish women in time of national rebuilding. "So, also, at the law giving at Sinai, God reckoned first of all on the faith and devotion of the women. So, also, the Jewish Nation has established the fact — and all our generations have inherited it — that in all the sins into which our nation has sunk, it has been the faithfulness of our women to their convictions and sense of duty which has preserved and nurtured the seed of revival and return."[315]

---

314. Rav Hirsch on *Vayikra* 23:43
315. Rav Hirsch on *Vayikra* 23:43. In a similar fashion, Rav Hirsch

A number of concepts and facts are compacted into these powerful statements, so some elaboration might be helpful. The reader's patience is asked if the elaboration gets a bit involved, but many ideas are at play here. Rav Hirsch alludes to righteous acts of Jewish women throughout our history, some of which came at moments of lapse in the spirits or divine service of many men. At the sin of the Golden Calf, the men, excepting the tribe of Levi, the leaders of the tribes, and some others,[316] responded to the nation's desperation over Moshe's absence by allowing a group to create a forbidden religious idol.[317] The women refused to contribute their jewelry for the manufacture of this idol.[318] As a reward, Hashem gave the women special halachahs and a special connection to *Rosh Chodesh*, making it something of a *Yom Tov* for them.[319] In Egypt, the oppressive workload of slavery induced the men to despair about the future, but the women consoled them and encouraged them to produce families.[320]

Our mothers have displayed righteousness throughout Jewish history. Their acts in the desert, at the receiving of Torah, and in Egypt should not come as a surprise. What is curious is

---

explains why Bris Milah applies only to the man (*Vayikra* 23:43). The *Malmid HaTalmidim* explains that Bris Milah, as a sign of the special elected status of the Jewish people before Hashem, does not apply to the woman because she is a helpmate to the man. In other words, her connection to the symbol of Milah comes through her marriage (*Malmid HaTalmidim, Parshas Lech Lecha*).

316. *Pirkei d'Rebbe Eliezer* 45.
317. *Shemos* 32:1-6.
318. *Midrash HaGodol* 32:2.
319. *Midrash HaGodol* 32:2.
320. *Midrash Abchir* as brought by *Torah Shelaimah* 1:151; *Meam Loez, Shemos* 1:15.

that the picture Rav Hirsch has drawn here may not seem a balanced view of Jewish roles. He has said that each gender performs a unique function. What is the male's part in the picture? For an answer, consider his words on the role and nature of the Jewish male.

> The male sex is *zachar*,[321] it is the depository of the Divine revelations and the spiritual attainments of the human race. To it has been entrusted the *zikaron*, the tradition of the human race as it has developed, in him is formed the spiritual chain which links together the beginning and the end of the human race; the male sex is the *zachar*, the bearer of history. Its activities do not belong wholly to the present moment, it has to think of the tasks and traditions received from God and from the past, and from the union of these with the events and conditions of the present to produce its own activities which carry on the chain of history further and further to perpetuity.[322]

So now, if the male's role is the bearing of the spiritual chain, what is the role of the woman, and how does it fit in with the original statements of praise about her?

> The female is the *nakeivah*...that which receives a vocation. The man chooses a calling, creates a position for himself, the women receives both by attaching herself to a man and entering into his calling and position. The girl blossoms into a woman, a Jewess, and only at the side of her husband does she at length acquire a separate existence, and the narrower sphere of activity

---

321. *Zachar* as a noun means "male" and as an verb means "to remember."
322. *Judaism Eternal*, vol. II, p. 51.

in which, united with her husband, she is called upon to perform her task as woman and Jewess in a definite calling and definite position. But just because the woman has not to acquire a calling and position for herself, she remains the nurse of all that is purely human in man. The great words with which the Father of humanity, as He fosters and watches over its development, announces its ultimate salvation and ingathering after all the mistakes it has made in the course of history are:... "God creates something new on earth, a woman encircles a man" (Jeremiah 31,21). The calling and position for which a man has to struggle are really nothing but the foundation on which he has to build his life's work, and carry out his own share in the general task of humanity. And there is a danger that he may completely lose himself in this struggle, that in striving to acquire the means he will lose sight of his real vocation and completely forget the great goal and his own task as a man, nay, that he will sacrifice and subordinate to these efforts what is genuinely human in himself. This is an error which can almost be regarded as the key to all the mistakes made in history. It is then the woman who leads him back to what is truly human in him.[323]

Hopefully, a fuller picture is emerging here. As mentioned earlier, the divine plan has devised it so that each gender has strengths which it shares with the other. The male has the awesome task of bearing the spiritual message for the world. This task, like any requiring intensity and vision, is vulnerable to its own energies. It needs a stabilizing force, something to keep it

---

323. *Judaism Eternal*, vol. II, pp. 51-52.

grounded or, when it stumbles or is slow to start, to help it to its feet. This is the job of the female. She is the "nurse" of the humanness in man. She is the helpmate in Hashem's image without whom the world would not endure, as it would not develop without the vision of man. Their effort, as has been said and will be said again, is that of a team, each member with a unique function.

Perhaps now Rav Hirsch's explanation of the exemption of women from positive time-bound commandments can be better understood. The woman's more faithful enthusiasm for her calling enables her to perform her role without the benefits of the positive time-bound commandments. She has an enthusiasm which may not function to lead the nation but protects and nurtures "the seed of revival" when reason has broken down in the nation. On the other hand, masculine spiritual qualities are suitable for the leading of the nation, but need the positive time-bound commandments for proper performance of the task.

For further explanation of Rav Hirsch, it may be helpful to consider a particular feature of his writing; namely his apparent attempt on many occasions to elaborate on particular aspects of the Torah in order to give encouragement towards Torah observance to his rather troubled generation. One should consider as well that Rav Hirsch's generation, despite its struggle with Torah, generally adhered to traditional understandings of the roles of men and women. Rav Hirsch's generation contrasts markedly with our generation which has peculiar views not only on the roles of men and women but on the natures, strengths and weaknesses of men and women as well. In view of these considerations and in view of the full breadth of Rav Hirsch's writings on this subject, it may be appropriate, in this author's view, to characterize Rav Hirsch's view on the exemption as follows: The female, in part due to the protection of the home environment and in part due to her nature, does not need the symbolic benefits of the positive time-bound commandments in order to fulfill her role. However, as the Maharal explains, the obligation of men in the positive time-bound commandments results from unique and positive spiritual attributes of the male personality.[324] It may be fair to say that the male has a spiritual nature which most productively utilizes the positive time-bound commandments to fulfill his role as bearer of the spiritual tradition of humankind. Rav Hirsch says that women have a greater enthusiasm for "their God serving calling." This enthusiasm enables the fulfillment of a women's invaluable role. However, this is not to say that a woman would have the same enthusiasm for the calling of the man. Indeed, it is the view of the Magen Avraham that she would not have such an enthusiasm.[325] The woman has one type of enthusiasm for divine service, and this enthusiasm works well with her role as mother and helpmate. However, it is one type of the many types of religious zeal which may occur and must occur in the religious journey of humankind. In other words, the female does not need these commandments to arrive at her destination, and the male needs the commandments to arrive at his. However, they are different destinations. As mentioned, these two paths of divine service combine to lift both man and woman to the highest path of living. Rav Hirsch may be presenting an example of such a relationship and its benefit to the world when he says, "Abraham's soaring spirit and Sarah's sense of propriety are the good angels which God has ordained for the rearing of mankind."[326] The miraculous success of Avraham and Sarah should be proof of the wis-

---

324. Maharal, *Tiferes Yisrael* 4.
325. *Zies Ra'anan* on *Yalkut Shemoni, parsha* 78 (*Shmuel* 1:1:18).
326. *Judaism Eternal*, vol. II, p. 63. Similarly, Shlomo HaMelech tells us, "a prudent wife is from the Lord" (*Mishlei* 19:14).

dom of this arrangement.

As suggested above, the support of the wife to her husband and her family serves the nation as well in times of national glory. We are told in Tehillim: "Happy is everyone who fears Hashem and walks in His ways. You shall eat the labor of your hands, and it shall be well with you. Your wife shall be as a fruitful vine in the innermost parts of your house, your children like olive plants around the table."[327] The mother's education of the children,[328] nurturance of spirituality and propriety in the home,[329] and support of her husband's learning[330] operate at all times. Note the many acts of lovingkindness by the *Imahos* in the building of the nation, the generous contributions by the women in the construction of the Mishkan,[331] and the sacrifices of Rachel, the wife of Rebbe Akiva, who lived twenty-four years apart from her husband while he toiled in Torah study.[332]

Rav Hirsch tells us also that the indispensability of women to Jewish life could put them on the forefront in times of national decline.

> Even in the times of decay the great influence which the Jewish woman from of old exercised in Jewish life can still be seen. In Isaiah chapters 3 and 4 the down-fall of the Jewish state is attributed principally to the fact that the women misused their influence. God enters into judgment with "the elders of His people and its princes", and -with the women! Both had completely misunderstood and misused their position; both had

---

327. *Tehillim* 128:1-4.
328. *Judaism Eternal*, vol. II, p. 92.
329. *Judaism Eternal*, vol. II, p. 54.
330. *Berochos* 17a.
331. *Shemos* 35:22; Ramban on *Shemos* 38:8.
332. *Nedarim* 50a.

exploited their influence for purely selfish aims, the great to satisfy their avarice, the "daughters of Zion" to satisfy their love of finery and luxury; they stepped forth haughtily and mincingly, they were the real "rulers" of the people. It was they who, according to Ezekiel, Chap. 13, gave the greatest encouragement to the lapse into idolatry and who worked themselves up into a prophetic ecstasy and became "hunters of souls" on its behalf. It was they who in the kingdom of Israel also, according to Amos, Chap. 4, by their management of affairs hastened the downfall of the state, and whose degeneracy, according to Isaiah, Chap. 4, had therefore amid the general collapse of all national virtues, first to be atoned for and removed before the nation could resume its God-fearing course of life."[333]

As Rav Hirsch adds, all this attests to the "high position and great influence" of Jewish women on the people and the dependence of the moral and social welfare of the nation "on the moral and spiritual elevation of the women."[334]

One should note that, while according to Rav Hirsch, a woman's role does not require the symbolic value of the positive time-bound commandments, it does seem to require the symbolic value of other commandments. This is implied in the parallelism between Rav Hirsch's discussion of the symbolic value of time-bound commandments and his discussion of a category of commandments called *Aidus*,[335] or Testimonies. According to

---

333. *Judaism Eternal*, vol. II, pp 85-86; Apparently from *Midrash Rabbah, Vayikra* 16:1; *Eichah Rabbah* 4:18; *Shabbos* 62b. See also *Shulchan Aruch, Even HaEzer* 17:2; *Kasav Sofer, She'elos U'Tshuvos, Orach Chaim, d'h VeAmar zal Adam echad.*

334. *Judaism Eternal*, vol. II, p 86.

335. *Aidus* are mentioned in a verse in *Devarim*: "And when your son

Rav Hirsch, *Aidus* are "Symbolic observances, monuments or testimonies to truths essential to the concept of the mission of man and Israel."[336] He says as well, "If a truth is to produce results, it must be impressed upon the heart and mind repeatedly and emphatically. This is the essential concept at the basis of Edoth [*Aidus*]."[337] Rav Hirsch's examples of *Aidus* include Shabbos, Yom Tov, Milah, Lulav, Tefellin, Tzitzis, Kiddush, *Havdalah*, *Chametz*, Purim, Chanukah, and Rosh Chodesh.[338] One may note that women are obligated in many of these commandments of high symbolic value.[339] One may note as well that a number of the *Aidus* incumbent on women are positive time-bound commandments.

It should be mentioned as well the observation of the *Chedvas Yaakov* that women are not exempt from positive time-bound commandments that are included in that group of commandments known as "between a person and his friend." Amongst the numerous ways of grouping commandments is a distinction of the commandments as focusing either on the relationship between a person and Hashem or on relationships between people.[340] Tefellin is considered a commandment "between man and Hashem." *Chesed*, or acts of lovingkindness,

---

asks of you in time to come saying what is the meaning of the Testimonies (*Aidus*), Statutes (*Chukim*), and Judgements (*Mishpatim*) which the Lord Our God has commanded you" (*Devarim* 6:20).

336. *The Nineteen Letters*, letter ten.
337. *The Nineteen Letters*, letter thirteen.
338. *Horeb*, section II, (*Edoth*).
339. The Ramban also defines *Aidus* as being symbolic. He describes them as "memorials to Hashem's wondrous acts." His examples of *Aidus* include Matzah, Succah, the *Korban Pesach*, Shabbos, Tfellin, and Mezuzah (Ramban on *Devarim* 6:20).
340. *Moreh Nevuchim* 3:35.

is considered a commandment "between a person and his fellow." The *Chedvas Yaakov* says that special verses are needed to exempt women from the commandment of giving the first fruits to the Kohen and from giving testimony in court because we might otherwise think that women are commanded in these. Even though they are positive time-bound commandments,[341] they are commandments "between a person and his friend," and would be incumbent on a woman.[342]

A few other explanations of the exemption of women from positive time-bound commandments will be discussed in the next chapters which focus on popular misconceptions on these subjects. The best way to close this chapter may be with the words of a sage who so brilliantly and piously worked to guide our generation in this and other matters. Rav Moshe Feinstein's responum on this subject incorporates in a compassionate and truthful manner many of the principles and views of the Rishonim and Acharonim. He said the following:

> ...the exemption of women from positive time-bound commandments is a decree of the Torah. Also, the Rabbis never obligated women in these commandments since there is no reason to do so. Indeed, there is a reason to exempt women from these commandments specifically for the reasons that the Torah exempts them. And besides the reasons of the Torah which are

---

341. The first fruits can only be given after a set period of growing time, and testimony cannot be given on Shabbos. For explanation see *Chedvas Yaakov* as referenced in following note.

342. *Chedvas Yaakov* 145:37 (As published in Pietrokow, p. 238) (Rav Tzvi Aryeh Yehudah Yaakov Maizlish, b. 19th century). *Olas Nidavah* adds that *Tzedakah* is a positive time-bound commandment since it cannot be given on Shabbos, and women are obligated in it (*Olas Nidavah*, p.133).

unknown to regular people and to the great scholars, and we are required to believe that there are great reasons of Hashem who gave the Torah, besides this, there are non-ultimate reasons revealed to everyone. In the matter of the exemption of women from positive time-bound commandments, the average woman is not wealthy and has responsibility to raise sons and daughters. This task is most important work for Hashem and His Torah, and so Hashem made each species so that the women should raise the offspring. Humans are no exception. The nature of women enables them to raise children. Along those lines, the burden was made easier on the women by neither requiring them to learn Torah nor to perform positive time-bound commandments.

However, even if the order of the world were to change and all the women were wealthy all the time and it were possible to give over the children to men and women to raise them as is done in our country, the Torah's law cannot change, and neither can that of the Rabbis. It is useless to fight this. Even with the agreement of the entire world, there is no power to change the Torah one iota. The women who stubbornly wage war to make such changes are committing heresy.

The Rambam, in chapter three, law eight, of the Laws on Repentance, says the following: "Three [people] are called heretics: The one who denies even one word spoken by Moshe Rabbeinu, the one who denies the explanation of the Oral Torah, and the one who switches one word [of Torah] for another. These are heretics, and their judgment shall be a forfeiture of their place in the next world. According to the words of the Rambam, to say that the Creator switches around commandments, and all the more so that men can switch around the commandments — is to say that the Torah is not eternal. And the whole reason [it is called heresy] is they are rebelling against many verses which teach us of the eternity of the Torah, and so writes the *Kesef Mishnah.*

Women are permitted to perform [certain] commandments for which they are not obligated and receive divine reward for such performance. And also according to the view of Tosfos, [women] are permitted to make a blessing [on such commandments] as is our custom. [It is our custom also for women to be permitted] to fulfill the commandments of Shofar and Lulav and to make blessings [on these]. Therefore, concerning Tzitzis, a woman who wants can dress in a garment not designed for men, as long as this garment has four corners to it, and attach Tzitzis to fulfill this commandment. Concerning the wearing of Tefellin, Tosfos writes in *Eruvin* 96, *divrei hamaschil: myachal*, that [this commandment] should not be performed [by women]. Tefellin requires tremendous care to keep the body in [halachic] cleanliness and to focus one's attention. For this reason even men who are obligated in Tefellin limit their wearing [of Tefellin] from all day to during morning prayers. The Rema holds similarly (*Choshen Mishpat* 98:3). *Targum Yonason*, on the verse: "There should not be a man's clothing on a woman" [holds] that [women should not wear] Tzitzis or Tefellin since they are garments of men. Tosfos does not believe there to be such a *Targum Yonason*. This [performance of non-obligatory commandments by a woman] applies only if her soul yearns to perform the commandment even though she is not commanded. [It is another matter] if her intention is to protest against the Holy One and his Torah. Such a posture is not congruent with the performance of a commandment. Indeed, it is a forbidden act and an act of apostasy since [such a woman] is trying to amend Torah law.

You should know that this the exemption of women from positive time-bound commandments is not because women are on a lower level of holiness than are men. While obligation in commandments results strictly from one's having holiness, men and women, in that sense, are equal in holiness.[343] All the verses in the Torah regarding holiness refer also to women. Therefore women also include in their blessings the words "you have sanctified us with your commandments." Women do this even when performing commandments for which they are not obligated. The exclusion of women from positive time-bound commandments is a leniency made by Hashem for his own reasons and not because of any diminution regarding women, Heaven forbid. We explained this earlier.[344]

Rav Feinstein's words in the foregoing paragraph appear to make a very telling statement about the nature of the exemption. Holiness brings a person to be obligated in commandments. In that regard, the equivalence in holiness between men and

---

343. It would appear from the context of the responsum and Rav Feinstein's writing style in general that he is referring to holiness in a halachic sense.

344. *Igeres Moshe, Orach Chaim* IV, 49.

women shows the connection of women to the positive time-bound commandments. The Gemara does not say that women are not obligated in the positive time-bound commandments. It says that women are *patur* or exempt from them. A person is usually exempt from a commandment to which he is ordinarily obligated. The language of the Gemara, as implied by the explanation of Rav Feinstein, shows some inner connection between women and the positive time-bound commandments. Women are exempted for reasons known only to Hashem and for the reason of household duties.

The responsum continues as follows:

> And concerning the obligations between husband and wife, a husband is obligated to treat his wife with respect, and a wife is obligated to treat her husband with respect. Furthermore many women were prophetesses and subject to the same laws concerning prophets as were the men prophets. In many matters, women were praised more than the men by the Written Torah and by the Rabbis. There is no denigration of women in their exemption from the learning of Torah and positive time-bound commandments. There is no reason to have any complaints.[345]

---

345. *Igeres Moshe, Orach Chaim* IV, 49.

Part III

Popular Misconceptions

"If [a person] merits [the Torah] is a medicine of life. If [he] does not merit, it is a deadly poison."

Yoma 72b

"There is perhaps nothing which has contributed in a greater measure to the diffusion and prevalence of wrong ideas and notions than the readiness of men to draw false or half-true conclusions from premises which in themselves are correct. Judgments which are right up to a point and can be rightly applied to certain persons and circumstances are given universal validity, and are tacitly allowed in men's minds to imprint themselves on conditions of a totally different character, in defiance of their own true scope and nature. Both natural science and historical and social studies suffer equally from this perversion of the reasoning faculty. The premises may be true, but not so the conclusions. And if these apparently logical conclusions are used as a welcome support for the fashionable notions of the day, they pass from hand to hand like coins, they form part of the public stock of ideas and views, they become well worn, and none takes the trouble to test them and to see whether their metallic content corresponds to their nominal value. The alloy many be the worst possible, but what does it matter? The coin is current, it serves its purpose, what more does one want?"

Rav Samson Raphael Hirsch
Judaism Eternal, vol. II, p. 49

Ten

Popular Misconceptions: An Introduction

As mentioned at the outset of this book, these subjects are not easy to sort out. The interplay of the strengths and vulnerabilities of men and women are rich and varied. What seems simple is often found upon closer analysis to be quite subtle. As *Mishlei* tells us, the words of the Torah are "like golden apples in silver-netted casings."[346] Viewed from a distance, one sees them as silver, but up close he sees them as gold.[347]

Additionally, the Rabbis make numerous statements on these subjects which seem to run at odds with one another. This approach is common in Torah literature. For example, the Torah commands us to "serve Him [Hashem] and to bind yourself to Him."[348] The Gemara asks about this command, "How can one bind himself to Hashem? Is it not written, 'The Lord your God is an all consuming fire.' "[349] The Gemara answers that our means of binding ourselves to Hashem is by emulating His attribut-

---

346. *Mishlei* 25:11.
347. Vilna Goan on *Mishlei* 25:11.
348. *Devarim* 13:5.
349. *Devarim* 9:3.

es.[350]

Such paradoxes call upon us to apply our minds and to come to higher understandings as a result of our efforts. An analogy from everyday life is the harp. If the strings of the harp are too loose, then any attempt to play them results in a dull thud or no sound at all. The music flows only from strings which are held in a state of healthy tension by anchors on opposite sides of the instrument.

In the expression of contrasting statements runs the danger of a person building his or her thinking on fragments of the complete story. Such is the dynamic early in the Chumash when Hashem says, "Let us make man."[351] We know clearly from numerous other statements of the essential Torah principle of Hashem's uniqueness as Creator and Ruler of the Universe.[352] Rashi tells us that nevertheless non-believers may try to use the verse as evidence against the uniqueness of Hashem, Heaven forbid.[353] Disregarding the designs of non-believers, the verse is phrased in the plural to teach the trait of modesty from the example of Hashem "consulting" with the angels before creating Adam.[354] The *Meom Loaz* comments as follows:

> The Holy One Blessed Be He wrote many things in the Torah which those lacking in sense can use to err and go after the ideas of non-believers. The reason that these are written as such is to allow for the giving of

---

350. *Sotah* 14a.
351. *Bereishis* 1:26.
352. *Shemos* 20:1. Consider also "Hear O'Israel, the Lord our God, the Lord is one" (*Devarim* 6:4). See *Derech Hashem* 1:1-6 and Rambam, *Sheloshah Asar Ikarim*, in the *Siddur* following *Shacharis*.
353. *Rashi* on *Bereishis* 1:26.
354. *Rashi* on *Bereishis* 1:26.

tremendous reward in the next world to the good children of Israel that see these words and conquer their
evil inclinations and work to interpret correctly.[355]

The obvious implication of this statement is the imperative for
the student of Torah to work with the full range of sources on a
subject.

As most of us know all too well, many outsiders to Torah in
recent generations have formed highly distorted impressions of
Torah views of the roles of women in Jewish life. The tragedy
for many people has been their stumbling upon sources which
require explanation in view of counterbalancing sources. On
other occasions, people are exposed to secular writings which
grossly misinterpret and unjustly misrepresent Torah sources.
Whatever the experience, it is incumbent on a person to seek out
the complete picture of Torah life which is after all a gift to us
from the omniscient and all-merciful Creator.

This book has dedicated a sizable portion of its discussion to
dispelling some of those distortions. As the points made in this
regard are distributed throughout the book, it may be useful to
summarize some of them here. One point is the ultimate equality
in worth of men and women as demonstrated by the creation
story. Adam, who was created in Hashem's image, was made
male and female. A second point is the inestimable value and
enjoyment of wifehood and motherhood and the causes for modern malignment of these roles. As a related idea, some explanation has been given as to the reason for distinction in roles
between men and women and why this distinction works for
everyone's greater sum benefit. A third point is the diversity of
women's roles as they manifest intellectually, emotionally, and
practically. A fourth point is the important role Jewish women

---

355. *Meam Loez, Bereishis* 1:26.

have played on a national level in times of crisis and the key role they regularly assume in contributing to national success. A fifth point is the ultimate similarity in the roles of men and women as servants of Hashem and physical beings on a spiritual mission. It has been pointed out as well the absurd modern devaluation of the fundamental and irreplaceable role of the man in family life and some of the causes for this dangerous trend. Furthermore, the dehumanizing social and financial pressures on men have been discussed and shown hopefully to be contradictory to life as guided by Torah.

Amongst additional misconceptions requiring attention are some which seem to have surfaced in recent years as an ironic result of attempts to draw people closer to the Torah. How this could come about is an interesting subject in itself as the next chapter will discuss.

Eleven

The Rationalization and the Prohibition

The temptation of assimilation into secular culture has been since the beginning of history one of the most difficult and perilous tests for Jews. Hashem warned our ancestors in the desert in the strongest terms to stay close to the Torah and to one another,[356] and the Jewish nation ever since then has received similar warnings from Hashem's prophets and sages.[357] Throughout the centuries, millions of righteous men, women, and children struggled courageously with the world and with themselves to hold fast to the proper course. Their divine reward, as well as their personal satisfaction, has been undoubtedly splendid.

Despite all of this, most of Jewry today, is massively assimilated to secular culture. This fact should come as no surprise to the reader as the problem of assimilation today is a painful matter for Orthodox Jews everywhere. What may come equally as

356. *Vayikra* 18:3; *Devarim* 7:3-4; *Shemos* 34:15-16.
357. For example, *Yermeyahu* 4:1-2; *Ezra* 10:10-11; *Nechemiah* 1:6-11; *Yesheyahu* 5:24; *Mishneh Torah, Hilchos Issurei Biah* 12:17; *Shulchan Aruch, Yoreh Deiah* 112, 113.

no surprise is the wave of return to Torah life and the outreach movement dedicated to enabling this return. The Torah commands us to reach out to others and help to bring them closer to the service of Hashem.[358]

But like any commandment, outreach to other Jews must be performed in conjunction with the many other commandments of the Torah. As the Mishnah says, "Be as careful in performing a minor commandment as a major one for you do not know the reward for each commandment."[359] This follows from the divine origin of commandments. What comes from the Almighty is infinite in substance. One piece cannot be compared to the next, nor can we know Hashem's real intentions behind His commandments. Accordingly, while the derivation and delineation of commandments is a primary focus of the Talmud, so too is the question of how the commandments are prioritized for differing situations. Proper handling of this complicated and subtle subject demands the brilliance and saintliness of our Sages who apply the Torah's guidelines to the issue. If the Sages give us general guidelines of conduct, one is wise to follow them regardless of whether he deems the other commandments better served through unsanctioned conduct.

Of particular challenge in fulfilling the commandment of outreach is keeping to the commandments concerning truthfulness. This is a natural by-product of the situation. In dealing with people who are struggling to understand Torah ideas, there is always a temptation to adulterate those ideas to win over the listener. But the verses tell us: "Keep far from a false matter"[360]

---

358. *Sefer HaMitvos HaKatzar, M'A* 3.

359. *Pirkei Avos* 2:1. See also *Berachos* 6b, where the Rabbis refer to "matters that stand in the heights of the universe but are regarded lightly by ordinary people."

360. *Shemos* 23:7. See *Kesubos* 17a for the connection of this verse to the prohibition of deceit in general (from *Horeb* 50).

and "You shall not steal, neither shall you deal falsely nor lie to one another."[361] In the Gemara *Kesubos*, Bais Shammai applies the prohibition even to lies in social situations made for politeness sake. [362]

Expressions of respect for truth are ubiquitous in Torah. The Midrash says that the world endures through truth, justice, and peace.[363] The Gemara tells us "The seal of Hashem is truth,"[364] and "Truth stands, but falsehood will fall."[365] We are taught that Yaakov Avinu's trademark was truth.[366] He set the foundation for the Jewish nation by combining Avraham's quality of mercy and Yitzchok's quality of justice to perfect the quality of truth.[367] Rabbeinu Bachya says, "Part of the concept of faith is that a person should love the truth. He should choose it [over falsehood] and he should speak it. As Zechariah the prophet said, 'These are the things that you should do: speak the truth, each man to his neighbor; execute the judgment of truth and peace [will be] in your gates.'[368]"[369] Rabbeinu Bachya says also,

---

361. *Vayikra* 19:11. Rav Hirsch explains that these commandments refer to the general prohibition against propagating untruths as well as to the more specific prohibitions against giving false oaths and false testimony concerning property (*Horeb* 50).
362. *Horeb* 50. See *Yevamos* 65b for discussion of the permissibility of making variations in expression in personal relations for the promotion of peace.
363. *Pirkei Avos* 1:18.
364. *Yoma* 69b; *Shabbos* 55a
365. *Shabbos* 104a.
366. *Micah* 7:20; *Sidur, Shacharis, U'Bolitzion*; *Michtav MeEliyahu* 3:155.
367. Rabbi M. Miller, *Sabbath Shiurim* (Gateshead: Gateshead Foundation for Torah, 5730), p. 59.
368. *Zechariah* 8:16.
369. *Kad HaKemach, Emunah*.

"Shlomo, may he rest in peace, said, 'The lip of truth shall be established forever.'[370] [Thus he] cautioned us to handle all our speech in accordance with the truth and to be careful [not to speak] falsehood."[371] He says as well, "All who are firm in the personality trait of truth, their prayers will be heard,"[372] and "The trait of faith stems from that of truth."[373] In the *Amidah* we ask Hashem to "give good reward to all those who trust in Your [Hashem's] name in truth."[374] Moreover, each one of us asks Hashem every day to "guard my tongue from evil and my lips from speaking falsehood."[375] In explanation of this prayer, Rav Shimon Schwab says, "This means that in our public and private lives we would not tell a *sheker* [a falsehood] even if it hurts; even if it hurts a lot!"[376] Moreover, Rav Schwab says the following:

> Hashem is the absolute *emes* [truth] and in the whole creation there is not one single creature which is not *emes* except the human being. We are the only exception! And to us is given the challenge to strive for *emes*. How can we have any hope of prevailing against the world of *sheker* [falsehood] if we ourselves are not meticulous about speaking nothing but *emes*....A new generation of *talmidei chachamim* [scholars] and *ovdei Hashem* [servants of Hashem] has grown around us. But we must realize that the world of *sheker* is also

---

370. *Mishlei* 12:19.
371. *Kad Hakemach, Emunah*
372. *Kad Hakemach, Emunah.*
373. *Kad Hakemach, Emunah.*
374. *Shemoneh Esrei, Tzadickim.*
375. Conclusion to *Shemoneh Esrei.*
376. Rav Shimon Schwab, *Selected Speeches*, Abridged Edition (NY: CIS Publishers, 1991), p. 173 (Rav Shimon Schwab, b. 20th century).

growing equally: intensifying its activities, waxing more militant and gaining more ground. There is only one option available to us: we must summon all of our talents to develop the power of *emes* to its fullest in every form, in order to give a final, fatal blow to the world of *sheker*.[377]

He says also, "*Klal Yisrael*, which is based on *Elokim Emes* [God of truth] and *Toras Emes* [Torah of truth], is also *emes*. *Emes* is exclusive! There is nothing besides *emes* except *sheker*. There is no neutral area, no middle ground, no place for compromise. If it is not *emes*, it is *sheker*!"[378]

In particular, one finds in the Torah severe admonitions against falsehood by scholars and educators. A Mishnah in *Pirkei Avos* says, "Scholars, be careful with your words, for you may incur the penalty of exile."[379] Rav Hirsch explains:

According to the Torah the penalty for accidental manslaughter was Galuth, exile in the form of enforced relocation to one of the Cities of Refuge. In this Mishna the "penalty of Galuth" is used with reference also to moral manslaughter, Scholars are warned against making rash or careless statements in their discourses that might cause the moral downfall of their disciples. They are cautioned against delivering themselves of utterances that are inaccurate, vague, or ambiguous and that may inspire erroneous views and result in spiritual and moral deviations from goodness and truth.[380]

---

377. *Selected Speeches*, pp. 173-4.
378. *Selected Speeches*, p. 170.
379. *Pirkei Avos* 1:11
380. *The Hirsch Siddur*, p. 426.

These words are a clear admonition against not only the teaching of patent falsehood but even of subtle falsehood, inaccuracy, and ambiguity. We must teach the truth and must teach it clearly. One finds another sharp message in the story of Akavyah ben Mehalel. He was promised the position of head of the court of Israel if he would alter his views on some controversial matters. He said, "Better that I be called a fool my entire life then be called an evil man for one hour by Hashem."[381] A clear message from these words is that one cannot veer from the truth for the sake of pleasing people.

An ever sharper message is found in the Maharshal. He comments on an incident where Torah was taught under threat of death to Roman government officials.[382] After the teaching, the officials expressed their satisfaction with the Torah except for the laws concerning fines to owners of oxen that cause property damage. These laws require more stringent standards of repayment for non-Jews than for Jews. The Maharshal comments as follows:

> Why did the Rabbis not fear that the evil kingdom [the Romans] would curse them? Could there be a worse thing to say before the nations than that we are exempt from [payment of] damages and they are obligated? Would it not be fitting to worry, Heaven forbid, about the many persecutions and destructions that have come from these people? Specifically, this evil kingdom's entire thought system was to precipitate the downfall

---

381. *Eduyos* 5:6.
382. *Baba Kama* 38a; Tosafos comments that laws forbidding the teaching of Torah to non-Jews (ie., the parts of the Torah which do not apply to them) do not apply if one is forced into the teaching by threat of death (Tosfos, *Baba Kama* 38a).

of its enemies. Accordingly, it would be for them [the Rabbis] to teach [these laws in an altered fashion making] either Jews and non-Jews obligated or both of them exempt. Rather, we learn from this of our obligation to give over [our lives] in sanctification [as opposed to altering the material]. And if, Heaven forbid, one alters the law he is an apostate [*cofer*] in the Torah of Moshe.[383]

The Maharshal adds that one need not volunteer controversial information in this life-threatening situation. However, truthful dissemination of the information, once requested, is considered a sanctification of Hashem's name. As the Chofetz Chaim tells us, sanctification of Hashem's name is a positive commandment from the Torah and if done in public is the highest possible deed.[384] From this powerful event, one cannot help but get a sense of the importance of truthfulness in the dissemination of Torah. And so the Mishnah says, "The one who interprets the Torah contrary to Halachah, even though he has accomplished learning and good deeds, there is no portion for him in the world to come.[385] Again, such a person has no portion in the world to come despite his learning and his good deeds. We must all take heed.

Despite all of these admonitions concerning truthfulness, a number of untruths about Torah are taught in outreach settings. A few of these have been touched upon in this book. Some of the teachings are exaggerations or oversimplifications of principles; others are patent falsehoods. Naturally, these mistakes do not blot out the wealth of good work done in outreach, but they can be substantial enough to harm the students and the commu-

---

383. Maharshal, *Yam shel Shlomo* 4:9.
384. *Sefer HaMitzvos HaKatzar, M'A* 3.
385. *Pirkei Avos* 3:11.

nity. The following chapters will focus on specific teachings concerning the roles and natures of men and women in Torah which tend to be given without sources and tend to contradict known authoritative views on the subject.

It should be added that motivations for bending of the truth are difficult to gauge on a case to case basis. Many people, perhaps most, may be somewhat innocently ignorant of referenced Torah views on these subjects. Of course, a person should know not to speak without knowledge, without researching the sources, or without consulting a Rav. As the Mishnah teaches, one of the seven qualities which can be said to characterize the wise person is that "on what he has not heard [in being asked a question on a Torah matter unfamiliar to him] he replies, 'I have not heard.' "[386] Similarly, the Talmud says, "Teach your tongue to say, 'I do not know,' lest you come to invent falsehoods."[387] Alternatively, some people may be intentionally offering altered views on Torah subjects for the alleged benefit of outreach. The rationale in such cases is usually that the listener will be better able to accept presently displeasing truths once he or she has tasted the beauty of Torah life. Certainly, one must use sense and sensitivity in deciding which materials are appropriate for beginners, but whether one may use falsehoods seems to be a whole different subject. As suggested by the plethora of Torah maxims on the imperative of truthfulness, the device of truth bending for outreach treads upon very dangerous territory.

Defenders of the latter approach often cite the famous principle that learning for impure motives leads to learning with pure motives.[388] One can respond to this rationale in a number of ways. The first is to cite Rav Eliyahu Dessler's explanation of

---

386. *Pirkei Avos* 5:7.
387. *Berachos* 4a.

the principle. Rav Dessler cites the teaching of Rav Simcha Zissel Sieff that learning with impure motives, for example, popularity, can come to learning with pure motives, for example, knowledge of Hashem's will, only if the person intends for his motives to improve. Otherwise, change does not occur.[389] How can a student who is told that untruths are truths have any sense of the impurities involved in either his motives or the teachings? Secondly, in the author's view, the principle is that impure motives lead to pure ones, not that falsehood leads to truth. There is a world of difference between the two ideas.

Interestingly, the Gemara cites a case in which a prospective convert approaches Shammai and asks him for a conversion so that he can become High Priest. Shammai rejects the man. By Torah law, only direct descendants of Aaron may become High Priests, thus excluding most Jews including converts. The man then approaches Hillel who does not comment on the validity of the man's claim but does move him along in the conversion process.[390] Some people have attempted to gain from this Gemara permission for manipulating Torah ideas for the sake of outreach. The author would like to argue against such a usage of the Gemara by pointing out the Gemara's particular features. Firstly, Hillel did not volunteer any misinformation to the prospective convert as some people in outreach will do. Rather, the man approached Hillel with the misinformation. Secondly, Hillel never tells the man that his misinformation about being a High Priest is correct information. Thirdly, the entire incident involves only a single individual. Teaching to groups is a differ-

---

388. *Pesachim* 50a.
389. *Michtav MeEliyahu* 1:24. For discussion in English, see *Strive for Truth*, vol. 1, pp. 96-100.
390. *Shabbos* 31a; the *Maharasha* says that the man was not converted at that time (*Maharasha* on *Shabbos* 31a).

ent matter as it presents special dangers. The author would like
to point out as well that Hillel was not teaching a fundamental
Torah principle but rather a small point which anyway would not
be relevant in a practical sense to his student for many years.
Moreover, in the Gemara's case, the student had harped on the
issue. Many of the incorrect teachings given over today in outreach are intended for people who have made no fuss over the
issues in question.

Twelve

The Spiritual Natures of Men and Women

The primary teaching to be considered here concerns the exemption of women from positive time-bound commandments. As has been explained, some people have experienced discomfort over this exemption, expressing a trepidation that women have been in some way left out of the main action of Jewish life. Hopefully, this book has achieved some success, with Hashem's help, in showing how the differing roles of men and women are equal in ultimate importance and opportunity for spiritual reward. Nevertheless, a common but invalid response to questions on the exemption has been to say that woman are exempt while men are obligated because in actuality women are higher spiritually than are men and not in need of the commandments. This matter has been touched upon[391] but now is an opportunity to delve into it in a more concentrated fashion.

Let it be said firstly that the motivation for taking up the subject is manifold. If nothing else, falsehood is dangerous, and it is incumbent on all of us to protect the integrity of Torah. As

---

391. See chapter eight.

Chazal say, "Do not say, we have elders for this, we have leaders and prophets. It is you, you who have to keep watch over the Torah. The Torah which Moses brought down to us is the inheritance of the community of Israel. You all stand before the Lord your God, the whole body of Jewish men, even the hewer of wood, and the drawer of water. Were you not all to step forward for the preservation of the Torah, then the Torah would perish."[392] One could propose that this is especially true in matters which can have repercussions on daily Jewish life. An invalid teaching on the roles and natures of men and women is a top candidate for such a repercussive matter. These repercussions will be elaborated upon throughout the next few chapters. Let the motivation for now be simply pursuit of the truth.

A number of recent books in English propose this idea of women's spiritual superiority over men, and reportedly, the idea is taught as well in numerous schools for women. The reader should note that none of the books in question offer a classical source for the idea, and none of several teachers of the idea have been able to supply a source when interviewed by this author and numerous individuals known by the author. A few books offer personal interpretations of verses and events. However, personal interpretations are not sources. Torah literature is built on rich language and metaphor. If channeled properly, these convey deep insight into life. However, one arrives at a different end if he approaches these materials with imagination unchecked by the discipline of traditional Torah scholarship. Indeed, the human imagination is potent. The *Akeidas Yitzchok* tells us that sin has its very origin in human imagination.[393] Accordingly, there could be theoretically no end to the production of wrong notions based on verses. The task is a function of

---

392. *Sifri* as brought by *Judaism Eternal*, vol. II, pp. 98-99.
393. *Akeidas Yitzchok, Bereishis, shaar* 9.

finding verses and exercising one's will upon them. Again, motives are not being questioned here, only the teachings themselves.

There are many logical flaws with the teaching of spiritual ascendency being based on obligation in fewer commandments. One of these flaws is the assumption that the sole purpose of commandments is to spiritualize insufficiently spiritual beings. Possibly, this assumption results from a misunderstanding of the principle that the 613 commandments correspond to the 613 limbs and vessels of the body. According to this principle, the performance of the commandment spiritualizes its corresponding body part. As was explained, no Jew is obligated in all 613 commandments and the spiritualization of our limbs and vessels occurs through our general acceptance of the yoke of Torah.[394]

In addition, the teaching contradicts a principle from the Gemara that commandments are placed on a person as a result of his having spirituality (as opposed to his lacking it). The Gemara in *Yevamos* ponders the existence of a special verse which commands *Kohanim* suffering from leprosy to shave their heads. A separate verse already makes such a command on the rest of the nation. The Gemara raises the possibility that the special verse is necessary because the special status of *Kohanim* may make inapplicable to them verses on commandments corresponding to other Jews.[395] The implication is that the extra holiness of *Kohanim*[396] works in conjunction with the commandments for *Kohanim*. These commandments are extra responsibilities which other Jews do not have. In other words, command-

---

394. Mabit, *Kiriyas Sefer, Hakdamah, perek* 7.
395. *Yevamos* 5a.
396. *Kad HaKemach, Kapparah* (near the beginning); *Bais HaOtzair*, 1, *M'A* 1-2, *Clal* 168 on *Yevamos* 56a as brought by *Mitzvas HaBayis* 1:7.

ments come as a result of holiness. The Maharal seems to apply this principle in his discussion of the exemption of women from positive time-bound commandments.[397] In that discussion, the Maharal analyzes the question of obligation in commandments from the perspective that spirituality is associated with obligation in increased numbers of commandments.[398] Rav Moshe Feinstein seems to have touched upon this idea in his responsum on this subject when he said "obligations in commandments result strictly from one's having holiness."[399]

Of course, the Torah frequently speaks about the function of commandments to thwart our potential for negative behavior by channeling it towards constructive acts.[400] For example, the Gemara says, "If that monster [the evil inclination] meets you, take him to the house of study,"[401] and "I have created the evil inclination, and I have created Torah as its antidote."[402] The Maharal explains that part of the function of Torah study is to allow men to channel their energy and aggressiveness in a productive fashion.[403] However, it would seem from the sources brought above that commandments are at least as much an expression of spirituality as they are a producer of it. It would otherwise have to be explained why the more a person grows in his or her divine service, the more commandment-related activity he or she takes on. It would have to be explained as well why the Jewish nation is responsible for a plethora of Torah commandments, and the nations of the world only a few.

---

397. See chapter eight.
398. *Tiferes Yisrael* 4.
399. *Igeres Moshe, Orach Chaim* IV, 49.
400. *Eruvin* 54a.
401. *Kiddushin* 30b.
402. *Kiddushin* 30b.
403. *Maharal, Derosh al HaTorah,* d'h *Shuv omar cah tomar.*

Therefore, it should not be surprising to find an abundance of classical sources which not only rebut the teaching of higher spirituality in women but explicitly state its converse. Among these sources are the Maharal,[404] the Taz,[405] the Magen Avraham,[406] the Shevet Mussar,[407] and Rav Tzadok.[408] This group consists of philosophers, *poskim* and Kabbalists, thus covering a broad range of disciplines.[409] It should be added as well that this author in his research for this book did not find any sources which put forth the idea of spirituality in women being on a higher level than that of men. Nor had any of the numerous *Gedolei HaTorah* interviewed for this book heard of any such sources.

----

404. *Tiferes Yisrael* 28; *Derech Chaim* 2:9 on Mishnah: *Amar Lehem Tzoo U'Rahoo, d'h U'mizeh*; *Chidushei Agados, Makos* 23b, *d'h U'mayatah*.

405. Taz, *Shulchan Aruch, Orach Chaim* 46 (Rav David HaLevi , b. 16th century).

406. *Zies Ra'anan* on *Shmuel* 1:1:13 (Rav Avraham Abale ben Chaim HaLevi Gombiner, b. 17th century).

407. *Midrash Talpiyos, Ohs Aleph, Anaf Ishah* (Rav Eliyahu ben Shlomo Avraham HaKohen, b. 17th century).

408. Rav Tzadok, *Dover Tzedek,* (Bnei Brak: Yahadus, 5727), p. 127 (Rav Tzadok Rabinowitz, b. 19th century).

409. See also *Lavush Techeiles, Hilchos Berachos* 46:5 (Rav Mordechai Yafeh, b. 16th century); *Akeidas Yitzchok, Shaarim* 6 and 9; Chidah, *Maris HaAyin, Shavuos* 18 (Rav Chaim Yosef David Azulai, b. 18th century); Baal HaTanya, *Payrush* on *Sheva Berachos,* last *berachah* (Rav Schneur Zalman, b. 18th century); Malbim on *Bereishis* 2:9, 2:18, and 2:21-22. These commentators seem to offer a similar view expressed in a less explicit manner. See also Rav Avraham Kook, *Olas Re'iah* on the *berachah sh'lo asani ishah* who expresses it explicitly. See also Arizal as brought by Ben Ish Chai, *Rav Pealim, Sod Yisharim* 10.

The Maharal, as shown before, teaches that the male nature has more *cochos hanefesh* or "powers of the soul."[410] He teaches also that female spiritual makeup leans more towards the physical aspects of spiritual life.[411] Again, none of this suggests unequal worth before Hashem, nor unequal value to the Jewish people. Both natures are invaluable. Each is designed to handle different aspects of Jewish life. Note the Maharal teaches as well that the female nature displays more tranquillity and that this tranquillity bears a parallel to that of the next world.[412] This, no doubt, is a very precious type of spirituality. However, a more exclusively spiritual leaning and a more highly charged type of spirituality are attributed to the male nature.

The Maharal spells this out in his explanation of the why Adam HaRishon was given commandments earlier than was Chava, but at the receiving of Torah, the women were approached before the men. The Maharal says that since in Gan Eden only part of the commandments were being given (rather than the full body of commandments) they had to be given to Adam. With only a partial set of the commandments, there is a less guidance and a higher possibility of coming to sin. Because of his higher spiritual level and closer connection to Hashem, Adam was in the best position to be entrusted with this partial set of commandments. Chava's eventual initiation of the first sin

---

410. *Derech Chaim* 2:9, *d'h U'mizeh.*

411. *Derech Chaim* 2:9; *Chidushei Agados, Baba Matzia* 59a; *Nasivos Olam, Hakdamah* (near the end); *Tiferes Yisrael* 4 and 28. See also *Nasivos Olam, Nasiv Avoda, sof perek* 3; *Be'air Hagolah* 3, *d'h VeChain* (page 47) and *Be'air Hagolah* 2, *d'h VeOde yesh lecha* (page 37). The Malbim expresses a similar view (Malbim on *Bereishis* 2:21-22) as does Rav Avraham Kook (Rav Kook, *Olas Re'iah* on the *beracha 'sh'lo asani isha'*).

412. *Derosh al HaTorah,* *d'h Shuv omar cah tomar.*

was indicative of her inability to work successfully with a partial set of commandments. At Har Sinai, since the full set of commandments was being given and there was less chance of one inventing improper modes of living, it did not have to be given first to the men.

> ...the man [Adam] was commanded first since his level was close to Hashem, may He be blessed. And because of this, the woman destroyed, since the connection of the woman to Hashem, may He be blessed, is not like that of the man....
>
> But Israel received a complete connection when Torah was given to them. And the proof of this is that Adam HaRishon received only a portion of the commandments, and therefore the connection was not complete but Israel, since the Torah given to them was complete, their connection to Hashem was complete. Therefore it is fitting for the woman to be commanded first at the receiving of the Torah since this thing was a complete connection. The woman was not at such a level when she received the decree but it was a complete connection. And afterwards the man was commanded. His connection and his level are greater than that of the woman. Therefore the command of the woman preceded that of the man.[413]

As the Maharal explains, given the decreased possibility of sin with a full set of commandments, it is better to approach the women first because of their eagerness for commandments. This eagerness is certainly a positive attribute but is a single attribute

---

413. *Tiferes Yisrael* 28.

which is not the sole component of spirituality.[414] As the Radal explains, the "eagerness for commandments" attributed to the women corresponds to a willingness to take on the yoke of commandments. However, the eagerness often fades when the obstacles to performing the commandments become burdensome. The Radal adds that the women in the generation of the desert were consistent in their commitment to commandments and not demonstrative of a fading in commitment in the face of obstacles.[415] The Maharal mentions other advantages to approaching the women first. These including encouraging them to raise their children in the ways of Torah[416] and teaching them of their equal sharing with their husbands of divine reward for their husband's Torah learning if the wives enable this learning.[417]

It should be useful here to repeat the words of Rav Hirsch who seems to refer to this "eagerness for commandments" when he describes the "greater fervour and more faithful enthusiasm for their God serving calling"[418] of Jewish women. And Rav Hirsch says as well that "in all the sins into which our nation has sunk, it has been the faithfulness of our women to their convictions and sense of duty which has preserved and nurtured the seed of revival and return."[419] Furthermore, the women of *Am*

---

414. *Tiferes Tzion* explains that the "eagerness in commandments" is necessary to counterbalance the destruction caused by Chava at the first sin. (*Tiferes Tzion* on *Midrash Rabbah, Shemos* 28:2). See *Tiferes Yisrael* 28 for a discussion of the spiritual dynamics of Chava's participation in the first sin.
415. Radal on *Midrash Rabbah, Shemos* 28:2:4 (Rav David Luria, b. 18th century).
416. *Tiferes Yisrael* 28.
417. Maharal, *Derosh al HaTorah*, d'h *Shuv omar cah tomar*.
418. Rav Hirsch on *Vayikra* 23:43.
419. Rav Hirsch on *Vayikra* 23:43.

Yisrael have refused to participate in a number of national sins. Perhaps most notable of these is the sin of the Golden Calf. The *Meom Loaz* comments:

> On account of this good act by the women, their refusal to give their rings for idol worship, the Holy One Blessed Be He rewarded them with a holiday to which the men have no portion. And it is Rosh Chodesh which they alone observe. And they also receive tremendous reward in the world to come.
>
> And they were given this holiday as a reward for not giving their rings for the Golden Calf. The holidays parallel the Avos. Pesach parallels Avraham, Shavuos parallels Yitzchok, and Succos parallels Yaakov. The twelve beginnings of the months of each year parallel the twelve tribes. Since the men sinned, the twelve beginnings of the months were taken away from them and given to the women. Thus it says in *Koheles* "One man of a thousand, I have found. And a woman from these I have not found."[420] At the sin of the Golden Calf, they [the men] said "These are your gods, Israel."[421] Not one woman sinned and said, "These are your gods Israel."[422]

Apparently, the *Meom Loaz* is connecting the word "these" from the verse in *Koheles* to that of the verse from the Chumash. Not a woman in a thousand was found to say "these", i.e., to participate in the sin of the Golden Calf. Rav Moshe Feinstein has said that "all the verses in the Torah regarding holiness refer also to

---

420. *Koheles* 7:28.
421. *Shemos* 32:3.
422. *Meom Loaz, Shemos* 32:3 (Rav Yitzchok Magriso, 18th century).

women" and "in many matters, women were praised more than the men by the [Written] Torah and by the Rabbis.[423] These comments of Rav Hirsch, the Maharal, the *Meom Loaz*, and Rav Feinstein do not seem to contradict the Maharal on this subject, nor do they contradict Rav Hirsch's own description of the Jewish man as the "depository of the Divine revelations and the spiritual attainments of the human race."[424] As mentioned numerous times, Hashem created men and women to carry different aspects of the monumentally challenging Jewish mission. The male is the more direct agent in transformation of the world to Torah values,[425] and the male nature is designed to provide the energy, activity, and insight which propels the Jewish people to higher religious service. However, the masculine nature needs to be accompanied by the stabilizing and nurturing aspects of the female nature. The tranquillity[426] and the "faithful enthusiasm"[427] of the Jewish female are ideal counterparts to the vigorousness of the male. Each side is making a religious contribution. There are numerous other ways of viewing the balance. Where the male role frequently focuses on intellectual abstraction,[428] the female role insures the intelligent handling of the concrete.[429] She also provides a special variety of wisdom built on intuitive understanding.[430] This intuition combined with nurturance help immeasurably to give Jewish life a warmth and a

---

423. *Igeres Moshe, Orach Chaim* IV 49.
424. *Judaism Eternal*, vol. II, p. 51.
425. *Maharasha* on *Baba Basra* 117a. See also *Judaism Eternal* vol. II, p. 51.
426. *Derosh al HaTorah*, d'h *Shuv omar cah tomar*.
427. Rav Hirsch on *Vayikra* 23:43.
428. Malbim on on *Bereishis* 2:21-2.
429. Malbim on on *Bereishis* 2:21-2.
430. *Niddah* 45b.

fullness.

This balance between the differing contributions and attributes of men and women can be seen in depictions of differing aspects of the formation of the first man and woman. On one side is the earlier maturity displayed by girls. As the Mishnah concludes, girls reach maturity at age twelve and boys at age thirteen.[431] Rav Hirsch seems to explain this dynamic as resulting from the respective sources of their creations.

> Our sages ascribe all the special characteristics of the female voice, the female character and temperament, as well as the earlier spiritual and mental maturity of women, as being connected with this formation of Woman out of the already feeling, sensitive, living body of Man, in contrast to Man, whose body was created out of earth.[432]

Thus the woman's formation from man gives her a certain head start in certain aspects of her development. It gives her as well certain personality characteristics which are uniquely feminine and no doubt of tremendous importance to the Jewish people. One should note that Rav Hirsch did not say that women are more spiritual, only that they are in possession of specific spiritual gifts and that girls sooner reach their unique adult maturity. The Mishnah upon which Rav Hirsch appears to base the latter part of his statement discusses the ages at which children reach adulthood.[433] While this Mishnah may hint at philosophical issues supplemental to the matter of adult maturity, the Mishnah by no means discusses spirituality in all its myriad manifesta-

---

431. *Niddah* 45b.
432. Rav Hirsch on *Bereishis* 2:21.
433. See *Nidah* 45b.

tions and levels."[434]

The manifestation of spirituality in men and women is symbolized by a different aspect of the creation which must be considered as well. As Rav Tzadok explains, a particular distinction between men and women stems from Adam's creation from Hashem's will alone and Chava's from a combination of the will of Hashem and the request of Adam. Adam asked for a wife after he had looked upon the natural world and observed that he was the only creature without a mate.[435] This shows that in addition to Hashem's infinitely pure will for Chava's creation was Adam's will which naturally must contain some human and earthly elements. The mixing of the wills of Hashem and Adam caused Chava to be created on a level less than Adam's.[436]

Combining these two depictions of the creation story we build a fuller picture of the characteristics of Adam and Chava, and by extension, masculinity and femininity. On one hand, Chava was formed from Adam, and Adam from earth. Thus the feminine generally experiences earlier development in certain aspects of basic spirituality. On the other hand, Adam was created from Hashem's will alone and Chava was created from the will of Hashem and the request of Adam. Thus, the masculine

---

434. Rav Hirsch says elsewhere, "While fully appreciating the special and deeply implanted characteristics of the female sex, the Sages also attribute to it complete spiritual and intellectual equality with the male (*Judaism Eternal*, vol. II, p. 95). It is difficult to determine the exact meaning of this statement since it is vague. Rav Hirsch has clearly detailed the differing roles of men and women, so it is likely that he speaks of an ultimate equality which is achieved through the differing paths.

435. *Meam Loez, Bereishis* 2:20.

436. *Dover Tzedek*, p 121. *Meam Loez* says, "Everything is influenced by the source from which it is created (*Meam Loez, Bereishis* 2:21-22).

generally experiences a more significant leaning towards higher spirituality. In sum, we see again a balance between the differing spiritual natures of men and women.

As a side point, the depiction of the formation of man from earth should not be taken as disparaging to men (or to women who come from men) as some have regarded it. Rav Hirsch tells us that "the material for the human body was its [the earth's] culminating and noblest product."[437] Prior to the creation of man, the earth had participated in the bringing forth of the various creations such as plant and animal life. However, the earth was passive at the creation of man and only prepared itself to be used for this most noble of creations. Additionally, the earth was used only for the earthly part of man. As Rav Hirsch says, "Human life, that which lives in Man, God did not take from the earth."[438]

Continuing the presentation of classical sources on the spiritual natures of men and women, the Taz, a main commentator on the *Shulchan Aruch*, cites his view on this general topic in his commentary on the blessing "thou has not made me a woman." He discusses why the accompanying blessings concerning the non-Jew and the slave are made in the negative ("thou has not made me" as compared to "thou has made me"). According to the Taz, the comparison to a different category of person, e.g., a non-Jew, demonstrates the worth of that category of people. It is better to be distinguished from something of value than something without value.[439] Following these comments, the Taz says the following:

When women make the blessing "thou has made me

---

437. Rav Hirsch on *Bereishis* 2:7.
438. Rav Hirsch on *Bereishis* 2:7.
439. Taz, *Shulchan Aruch, Orach Chaim* 46.

according to His will," a blessing not in the Gemara, it goes well with what was written before [that these blessings are made as thanks for distinction from groups with positive attributes]. Behold, we see in the blessing of the man that [his attributes] are above the creation of the woman. Therefore, it is fitting that she make a blessing on her positive attributes.[440]

In other words, she makes a blessing in view of her significant positive attributes, but must make it in the positive form ("thou has made me") because there are no groups left from which to distinguish her. She has already said the blessings concerning the non-Jew and the slave. To make a blessing on her fine qualities, she must make it in the positive. The man, whose general level exceeds hers, can make the blessing in the negative.

It may be appropriate to explain the words of the Taz with a comment attributed to Rav Aharon Kotler about the difference between being a full-time scholar and being a *baal habayis*.[441] One version of the story says that Rav Kotler was asked to comment on which life of the two is better. Rav Kotler is reported to have said that in the next world, the two are the same. That is to say, that the *baal habayis* who supports others in learning and himself dedicates his time away from work to learning can earn as pleasurable a place in the next world as the full-time scholar. (One can assume application of the Ramchal's premise that the *baal habayis* be involved in his trade "out of necessity" and not out of acquisitiveness.) However, Rav Kotler adds, in this world, full-time immersion in Torah is a sweeter life. Similarly, it may be that the man thanks Hashem for endowing him with a special

---

440. Taz, *Shulchan Aruch, Orach Chaim* 46.
441. Translated in this context as a person with a full-time occupation who can only dedicate after-work hours to learning Torah.

spiritual nature which allows him to fulfill more types of commandments. As a side note, the lives of all Jews have the potential to be enormously sweet and rewarding in accordance with the verse "It's ways are ways of pleasantness."[442] The story brought here speaks of subtle dimensions of certain aspects of life. As for the possibility of joyful living, the Chazon Ish says, "When a person's mind merits to see the truthfulness of the reality of Hashem, he is immediately filled with an unlimited ecstasy."[443] He says as well, "The essential life of man stems from the breaking of his negative character traits. The righteous have a hold on their inclinations rather than their inclinations having a hold on them. Is it not the greatest delight and the sweetest pleasure to rule over one's animal spirit? It brings constant happiness and it restores one's soul."[444] One more note, the reference to the sweetness of immersion in Torah should not be taken to mean that the scholar's life is an easier life. As mentioned earlier, the learning of Torah is a challenging and arduous activity. As the Talmud tells us, the verse "For man was born to toil"[445] is a reference to Torah study.[446]

The reader should note that throughout Jewish history, the great majority of men have not had the opportunity to engage in full-time learning.[447] Distribution of opportunity for experience in this world is not necessarily equitable in every respect. However, the most pleasurable opportunity of all, to serve Hashem on His terms, is equally available to all. And the oppor-

---

442. *Mishlei* 3:117.
443. Chazon Ish, *HaEmunah VeHaBitachon* 1:9 (Rav Avraham Yesheyahu Karelitz, b. 19th century).
444. Chazon Ish, *Collected Letters*, vol. II, 13.
445. *Iyov* 5:7.
446. *Sanhedrin* 98b.
447. See Chidah, *Maris HaAyin, Berachos* 17.

tunity for eternal reward, which infinitely outshines temporal pleasure, is equally available to all. The Gemara tells a story of a son who reported to his father a dream where he saw what he called "an upside-down world." In this upside-down world, many of the people who were in the most disadvantageous positions in our world fared the best. Additionally, many of the people who fared best in our world were in the worst positions in the upside-down world. The father told his son, "In your dream you were not seeing an upside-down world; you were seeing the real world."[448] What all this may mean is that Hashem created the world with a certain spiritual and social structure just as he created a physical structure. Our place within that structure is but one manifestation of our lives. The way we handle ourselves within that structure is a better determinant of our true standing in the world.

This dynamic is demonstrated in a story involving David HaMelech and Yerovam Ben Nevat. Hashem told Yerovam Ben Nevat of Hashem's vision of Himself, Yerovam Ben Nevat, and David HaMelech walking in the Garden of Eden — in that order.[449] Yerovam Ben Nevat had to walk behind David, the King of Israel, in this world. But for walking behind him in this world, he would be rewarded by walking so close to Hashem in the next world. Unfortunately, Yerovam Ben Nevat failed to manage the task.[450] But the outcome was highly successful for Eliezer, the servant of Avraham, who remained true to his calling and his place in the nation of Israel. As the Midrash says about Eliezer, "Because he served that *Tzaddik* [Avraham] faithfully, he went from the category of accursed to the category of

---

448. *Baba Basra* 10b.
449. *Sanhedrin* 102a.
450. *Sanhedrin* 101a.

blessed."[451] So too it went for Aaron, the older brother of Moshe, who readily and happily deferred to his younger brother's leadership.[452] So too was the outcome splendid for Sarah, Rifka, Leah, and Rachel, our glorious mothers, who fulfilled their tasks as commanded by Hashem. It should be interesting to add that Miriam, who as well fulfilled her life's goals primarily in traditional fashion,[453] is said by the Rambam to be one of the three people who left this world through the gentlest cause of a kiss by Hashem. According to the Rambam, this manner of worldly departure is indicative of superlative transcendence of one's physical nature in such a manner as to allow for consistent experience of extremely elevated knowledge of and love for Hashem.[454] The other two people to have passed on in such a manner are Moshe Rabbeinu and Aaron HaKohen.

Among the other authorities in our original list is the *Zies Ra'anan*, otherwise known as the Magen Avraham, who was a chief commentator from the sixteenth century on the *Shulchan Aruch*. The *Zies Ra'anan* interprets the *Yalkut Shimoni*, on the verses in *Shmuel*[455] which describe Channa's prayers to be blessed with children. The Midrash says, "Why were women classified with minors and slaves with regard to commandments: Because they have but one heart, as it is written, 'And Channa said in her heart.' "[456] According to the *Zies Ra'anan*, the meaning of the Midrash is that the good inclination does not dwell in women to enough of a degree as to obligate them in the positive time-bound commandments.[457] He says that if they were com-

---

451. *Midrash Rabbah, Bereishis* 60:7.
452. *Akeidas Yitzchok, Shemos, shaar* 35.
453. See *Bereishis Rabbah, Shemos* 1:19-20.
454. *Moreh Nevuchim* 3:51.
455. *Shmuel* 1:1:13.
456. *Yalkut Shemoni, Shmuel* 1:1:13.
457. *Zies Ra'anan, Yalkut Shemoni, Shmuel* 1:1:13. The verse in

manded, it is probable that they would not fulfill the obligations and are therefore exempted from them.

Rav Ovadia Yosef expresses discomfort with the interpretation of the *Zies Ra'anan*. Rav Yosef questions how the verses in question, which portray a positive deed by Chana, can be interpreted as a reference to the negative inclination. He proposes instead that the reference to "one heart" indicates a kind of inspiration, or *cavanah*. Rav Yosef's proposed connection of this reference to the reference to the exemption of positive time-bound commandments is vague; although it is somewhat reminiscent of Rav Hirsch.

> It appears that the intention of the Midrash is that therefore they are not in need of the positive time-bound commandments. It is enough for them to turn their hearts to their Father in Heaven with prayer and commandments that are relevant to them.[458]

What Rav Yosef seems to be saying essentially is that the positive time-bound commandments are neither congruent to the female nature nor to the woman's role. However, his exact meaning is not clear. As mentioned, Rav Yosef may be offering a view similar to Rav Hirsch. According to that view, a woman's lack of need for those commandments is a function of several interacting factors. These factors are the woman's general historic isolation from the negative influences of the marketplace and her initial enthusiasm for commandments (or in Rav Yosef's

---

Shmuel spells "her heart" with a single letter *bais* unlike the verse in *Devarim* (*Devarim* 6:5) which spells 'your heart' with two such letters. Rashi (Rashi on *Devarim* 6:5) tells us that the spelling with two letters in *Devarim* indicates a reference to the two inclinations: good and evil.

458. *Yabia Omer* 40:9 (Rav Ovadia Yosef, contemporary).

terminology her *cavanah,* or inspiration). These factors render her unneeding of the positive time-bound commandments in order to fulfill her role. One must note that, of course, the man has a different role. Rav Hirsch has called the man the bearer of the spiritual tradition.[459] While the trait of initial enthusiasm for commandments (or *cavanah*) in part renders a woman unneeding of these commandments to fulfill her role as mother and helpmate, the spiritual qualities of the man render him fitting for these commandments[460] to fulfill his role as bearer of the spiritual tradition. This is why the woman does the commandments which Rav Yosef describes as "relevant to her" and the man does those relevant to him. Obviously, commandments have many functions which will fit into our lives in different ways. As mentioned earlier, sometimes they inspire spirituality, sometimes they engage our spirituality. It is difficult to clearly decifer the words of Rav Yosef due to their brevity.

Among some of the other commentators, the Shevet Mussar, a great kabbalist from the seventeenth century, explains the distinction in the spiritual levels of men and women as resulting from intellectual orientation.

> The man rises above the woman in the totality of things, as his refined intelligence grasps the wise and spiritual matters.[461]

In the passage, he then embarks on a kabbalistic discussion and attributes to the male the qualities of fire and air, and to the woman the qualities of earth and water. He then says that these qualities of the man parallel the substance of the heavens and enable him through intellect to penetrate great spiritual worlds.

---

459. *Judaism Eternal,* vol. II, p. 51.
460. Maharal, *Chidushei Aggados, Makos* 23b, *d'h U'mayatah.*
461. *Midrash Talpiyos, Os Alef, Anaf Ishah.*

What the Shevet Mussar seems to have alluded to here is a variety of intellect more commonly attributed to the male nature. It would seem that the male nature in general has a type of intellect which lends itself well to contemplation of Torah. The Malbim explains this distinction in types of intellect through the story of the creation of the first man and woman. The woman was built from part of Adam while Adam slept.[462]

> Hashem wanted Adam to use only his speculative intellect and Chava to use her practical reason. Accordingly, [He] gave [Adam's] share of practical reason to Chava. Therefore Chazal say that [the verse] "He built" alludes to *binah* [understanding], since [He] gave more understanding to the woman than to the man with regard to basic intellect. Thus it was necessary to make Adam sleep [as Chava was built] because the speculative intellect does not function then. As Chava was separated from Adam's body, she did not receive a share of the speculative intellect since it was asleep then. [She] received the applied reason.[463]

The Malbim says also that the applied intellect and practical understanding of the woman enable her to raise children and take care of the home, thus freeing her husband to study Torah.[464] The Malbim has also said that a chief function of the woman is to be a companion to the man.[465] We can imagine that intelligence is most relevant to her managing that task as well.

We may observe that the Malbim's commentary here

---

462. *Bereishis* 2:21-22.
463. Malbim on *Bereishis* 2:21-22.
464. Malbim on *Bereishis* 2:19:20. A similar idea is presented by the Abarbanel on *Bereishis* 2:18.
465. Malbim on *Bereishis* 2:18.

describes that both man and woman received *seichel* or, loosely translated, "ability to think." The question at hand concerns the differences in their respective orientations toward thinking. Additionally, numerous sources have been brought throughout this book to verify the potential for exercise of abstract intellect in women's general roles in Torah life.[466] Thus, the words of the Malbim should probably not been taken as a purely dichotomized depiction of the differing intellectual orientations of men and women. Nevertheless, his words do describe a significant distinction in the modes of thinking of each gender. His words describe as well the ramifications of that distinction and, accordingly, appear to enlighten us as to the meaning of the Shevet Mussar on this chapter's subject matter. It should be repeated as well the point of the Rambam that philosophical teachings in Torah outline the majority of cases. They do not attempt to describe all people in all situations.[467]

If the author may suggest another idea as well, one may wonder how much of our spiritual and intellectual natures are inborn and how much they develop from the roles we assume. It is very hard to define what people are. When the Torah describes the characteristics of masculinity and femininity, it may be speaking largely about the generic energies within all of us and the particularized development of these energies through our roles. In other words, masculinity and femininity are attributes within all people.[468] We each develop particular components of

---

466. See, for example, *Akeidas Yitzchok, shaar* 9:7-8 who says that such an opportunity certainly exists for a woman, and that it comprises a higher divine service for her. However, such activity must work in concert with her role as helpmate for it to be of the kind encouraged by the Torah.
467. *Moreh Nevuchim* 3:34.
468. See *Vilna Gaon* on *Mishlei* 10:1: "The wise son is the happiness

those attributes through our roles. The Torah proscribes these roles so that Jewish life can proceed along a consistent and productive course. Accordingly, the halachah is binding on all people whether or not it seems to always fit comfortably with our estimations of our personal situations.

In further explanation of this point, it should be stressed that the Torah is given as much to the community as it is to the individual. As Rav Hirsch says, "It is not to the individual, but to the community that God entrusted His Torah as an inheritance for all the generations to come. For this reason, every individual is duty-bound to join forces with his community in thought, in word and in deed and loyally to share in its tasks and obligations, so long as that community proves to be a faithful guardian and supporter of the Torah."[469]

Of course, the success of the nation benefits the individual. As Rav Hirsch says:

> For the collectivity alone is strong, the totality alone is immortal even in this world. Therefore, by joining your own feeble energies to those of all, by letting mature the most beautiful fruits of your own endeavors for the benefit of all (for the union of individual energies, that is, the collectivity), you will become a great force for the supreme good, whose existence, far beyond your

---

of his father and the fool is the worry of his mother." On this verse, the Vilna Gaon says, "A man has two qualities, the quality of his father and the quality of his mother." He explains further that a man's job is to cause the quality of his father to predominate. Vilna Gaon on *Mishlei* 10:1 as dictated (see Introduction to *Sefer Mishlei im Pirush HaGra* [Tel Aviv: Petach Tikva, 5750]) to his *talmid* R. Menachem Mendel Bendit (b. 18th century). See also *Chaf HaChaim, Orach Chaim*, vol. I, *Hilchos Tefellin* 38:8.

469. *The Hirsch Siddur, Pirkei Avos* 2:5, p. 436.

own brief span of life, you will assure.[470]

Applying Rav Hirsch's words, this author proposes that our halachically prescribed roles provide for us, amongst their many other benefits, a means to connect and contribute to the nation. And, as mentioned many times, these different paths of divine service, the different roles, are all fulfilling. They are as well more multifaceted than many people understand them to be. However, this entire discussion is most speculative and difficult to ground firmly in classic sources. It is as well subtle and easy to misunderstand. Hence, it is mentioned here only in passing.

In further explanation of the words of the Shevet Mussar, it may be useful to repeat Rav Hirsch's statements from chapter six that the woman shares in the calling of the man by attaching herself to him.[471] The concept is no doubt discordant with some contemporary secular attitudes, but it would be to our detriment to hide the concept. If the divine plan establishes a relationship of principal and helpmate then it is in our interest to know it so that we may utilize it. As the Maharal tells us, when the woman enables her husband's Torah learning, she receives a reward equal to or perhaps greater than his.[472] Her sense of personal satisfaction from bringing such good to the world is likewise immense. The means of her work, being bound up in family and lovingkindness, suits the inner nature of women and the deep interest the great majority of women have in matters of love and relationships. It is a beautiful plan, whereby, in a manner of speech, the man and wife together journey to the heavens. In fulfillment of the commandment of *Limud Torah*, he focuses primarily on intellect, and she on emotions. Of course, the manifes-

---

470. *Horeb* 597.
471. *Judaism Eternal*, vol. II, p. 51.
472. *Derosh al HaTorah*, d'h *Shuv omar cah tomar*. See also *Aruch HaShulchan, Yoreh Deiah* 246:20.

tations of these principles in everyday life assume myriad forms depending on the exact natures of the people involved. As said before, his role does not exclude emotion, indeed emotion is a vital part of his existence, and the same may work for the woman and intellect. It is just that his primary involvement with the commandment of *Limud Torah* bears an intellectual tenor and hers an emotional one.

It should be pointed out that just as the woman draws close to her husband largely through her focus on him, the husband draws close to his wife largely because of her invaluable assistance to him.[473] This can be seen in the depiction of the creation of Chava, who was created in such a way as to cause Adam to appreciate her. Placed between the verses declaring the creation of the first person as male and female and the verses describing the making of the first woman is a description of Adam's naming of the animals: "The man gave names to every animal, to the birds of the sky, and to every beast of the field. But the man did not find a helpmate opposite him."[474] *Meam Loaz* describes the significance of this placement of verses:

> When Adam HaRishon saw that all the creatures of the world were made male and female he was anguished to see himself alone. He complained and said, "Why did you give each a partner but left me without a partner." The Holy One Blessed Be He fulfilled his request and said, "It is not good for man to be alone."[475]

---

473. Additionally, she has a natural desire for his companionship. This is evidenced in statements of Chazal such as "More than a man wants to marry, a woman wants to be married" *(Yevamos* 113a) and "Better to dwell in grief, then to live like a widow" *(Kiddushin* 41a).
474. *Bereishis* 2:20.
475. *Meam Loez, Bereishis* 2:21:22.

Adam requested to have a partner. Prior even to the formation of woman, Adam felt an appreciation for her.[476] And, as the Abarbanel says, the interdependence between man and woman is immeasurably more involved by humans than by other creatures, so the bond between them is likewise stronger.[477]

According to the *Akeidas Yitzchok*, the bond between husband and wife stems from the formation of Chava from the side of Adam.[478] As the verse says, "This is now bone of my bones and flesh of my flesh. She shall be called woman because she was taken from man."[479] Similarly, the *Payrush Maharzav* tells us that man's heart is drawn towards his wife since she was taken from him in this manner.[480] She is a part of him. Interestingly, the *Shulchan Aruch* seems to echo some of these thoughts in its detailing of some of the laws concerning appropriate situations for recitation of *Krias Shema*. Under certain circumstances, a husband may recite *Krias Shema* while in close physical proximity to his wife (and vice versa) because the wife is, in the words of the *Shulchan Aruch*, *k'goofo,* or like his body.[481] Their relationship enjoys such an intimacy that close physical proximity does not breach the normal rules concerning physical division between men and women in prayer.

The husband is also drawn to love of his wife in his appreci-

---

476. *Chaim shel Osher* 1:67. (For discussion in English, see *Fulfillment in Marriage* 1:58.)
477. *Abarbanel* on *Bereishis* 2:18.
478. *Akeidas Yitzchok, Bereishis, shaar* 8. He adds that Adam was made to sleep during the formation of Chava so that he would rejoice in surprise at finding her when he awoke.
479. *Bereishis* 3:23.
480. *Payrush Maharzav, Midrash Rabbah, Bereishis* 17:7 (Rav Zev Einhorn, 19th century).
481. *Shulchan Aruch, Orach Chaim* 73:2. See also *Menachos* 93b.

ation for her assistance to him.[482] *HaCaras Hatov* or appreciation for the good done to us by another is a building block of Jewish life. Adam was sent out of the Garden of Eden because of the ingratitude he displayed when he blamed his wife for his eating of the forbidden fruit. She had given him the fruit, but she was also a gift to him from Hashem, and his complaint showed a lack of appreciation.[483] One reason for this emphasis on gratitude is that the trait of appreciation leads to appreciation and recognition of Hashem. Ingratitude produces blindness to Hashem. As the Midrash says, "A person begins by failing to acknowledge the good received from his friend, and the next day he will come to ignore the beneficence of his Creator."[484] It is imperative for a person to train himself to recognize his dependence on others and to feel and show appreciation for the good received from others. Needless to say, this applies as well to the wife as her husband guides her in the ways of Torah,[485] joins with her in the rearing of children, shows her love, supports her financially,[486] and gives to her in myriad other ways as well.

---

482. See *Yevamos* 63a; *Avodah Zara* 5b; *Vilna Goan* on *Shir HaShirim* 5:2.
483. *Akeidas Yitzchok, Bereishis, shaar* 9
484. *Mishnas Rebi Eliezer* 7.
485. *Akeidas Yitzchok, Bereishis, shaar* 9; *Judaism Eternal*, vol. II, p. 58.
486. *Meam Loez, Bereishis* 12:8.

Thirteen

The Sin of the Golden Calf

Feeding into the popular misconceptions concerning the spiritual natures of men and women are a number of narrower topics, some historical, some philosophical which should be discussed as well. Of historical interest is the sin of the Golden Calf and other sins committed by Israel in the desert after the Exodus from Egypt. People are sometimes heard to say that the refusal of the women to participate in the making of the Golden Calf is evidence of women's higher spirituality. One can see how such a view is contradicted in a general sense by the numerous authorities brought in the last chapter. It may help also to tackle the logic of the misconception and show its fallacy in that way.

The question of how Israel could involve itself in the making of the Golden Calf is much discussed amongst the great scholars. The pivotal question, oftentimes, is how could the nation commit this act only forty days after the revelation at Sinai.[487] A recurring theme amongst the numerous approaches offered on the subject is that the sin of the Golden Calf was very much a function of the highness in the spiritual level of the peo-

---

487. *Bais HaLevi, Parshas Ki Sisa* (Rav Yosef Ber Soloveitchik, b. 19th century).

ple, not of a lowliness, Heaven forbid. For example, the Ibn Ezra and the Ramban engage in a lengthy debate over the intentions of the nation in committing the sin.[488] Both commentators agree that the nation sought to adapt itself to its spiritual precariousness in Moshe's absence. The exact analysis of each commentator is not relevant here. What is relevant is their shared premise that the nation strove to maintain its spiritual level in Moshe's absence. Their act was a grave sin, but the sin of inspired and highly spiritual people. As the Ibn Ezra says, "Heaven forbid, Heaven forbid, that Aaron should make an idol, or that Israel would want an idol. Rather, they thought Moshe was dead....When they did this it was with the intention of honoring Hashem....However, the mixed multitude influenced them....And a few of the Jews thought it was an idol...The number that thought of it as an idol was less than three thousand. This is less than a half of one percent of the camp."[489]

Pursuing the point from another angle, Rav Dessler shows how the sin of the Golden Calf was only considered a sin by virtue of the high level of that generation. According to Rav Dessler, the making of forms for religious symbolism is actually sanctioned in some situations, as, for example, the manufacture of the Bronze Serpent.[490] The making of the Golden Calf was considered a sin for the people of that generation because their high level at the time should have rendered them transcendent of such symbols. As Rav Dessler says, this explains the statement of the Rabbis: "[The generation of the desert] never committed a

---

488. *Michtav MeEliyahu* 1: 273-277.
489. Ibn Ezra, *Shemos* 32:1 (Rav Avraham ben Meir ibn Ezra, b. 12th century). For discussion in English, see *Strive for Truth*, vol. III, "The Golden Calf."
490. *Bamidbar* 21:8-9.

real sin, nor did they ever undergo a complete punishment."[491] Some of their actions were considered sins because people on such a high level are held to a higher standard.[492]

The *Bais HaLevi*, like other commentators, says that the nation's intention with the Golden Calf was to maintain its closeness to Hashem in Moshe's absence. The construction of the calf was an attempt to build a dwelling place for the Divine Presence, much like that later accomplished by the sanctuary. Their mistake, says the *Bais HaLevi*, is that such an act must be commanded by Hashem for it to be successful.[493]

Moreover, the *Bais HaLevi* says that the deep spiritual awareness of the people enabled them to attempt the construction. In other words, it was a mistake of high intellect. Accordingly, the Chumash describes the gold covering on the ark as an atonement for the sin. The gold cherubim, which sit upon the ark, symbolize the nation's attachment to Hashem, an attachment which results from Torah study. Intellect channeled constructively is the atonement for the sin of the Golden Calf because it was a sin of intellect.[494]

In view of these comments of the *Bais HaLevi*, one can understand why the sin of the Golden Calf was precipitated by the men. Intellectual leadership in spiritual matters is the men's responsibility,[495] a function of special spiritual qualities within men.[496] The sin of the Golden Calf by no means denotes less

491. *Yalkut Shemoni, Beha'alotcha* 732 as referenced in *Michtav MeEliyahu* 1: 273-277.
492. *Michtav MeEliyahu* 1:162.
493. *Bais HaLevi, Parshas Ki Sisa.*
494. *Bais HaLevi, Parshas Ki Sisa.*
495. *Baba Matzia* 59a; Maharal, *Chidushei Agados, Nidah* 45b; *Akeidas Yitzchok, Bereishis, shaar* 9; *Judaism Eternal*, vol. II, p. 58.
496. Maharal, *Derech Chaim*, 2:9; Malbim on *Bereishis* 2:20. See also

inclination toward spirituality on the part of the men, but may indicate a spirituality which can get off course. One is reminded of Rav Hirsch's comments from chapter nine that men bear the spiritual mission but may lose themselves from time to time in that mission. Jewish women protect and nurture the seed of revival. What the women offer is not a greater spirituality but a spirituality which sometimes takes the safer course. The sin of the Golden Calf was such a case.

This concept of great sins coming from great people is a fundamental of Torah thought. Some of our greatest saints were people who stood at one point in their lives at great distances from Torah life. Reish Lakish, a prominent voice in the Gemara, was at one time a bandit.[497] Rabbi Akiva, whose scholarship and piety were of the highest order,[498] said that as a youth he was so hostile to Rabbinical authorities that he would like to have taken a Rabbi and bitten him with the hard bite of a donkey.[499] The principle is well demonstrated as well in the story of Abaye who made an interesting observation about himself after accompanying a young man and woman on a walk. After completing the walk, the young man and woman parted ways without making any exchange of physical affection. Rav was troubled by his sense that he in a similar situation would not have withstood temptation. An old man offered him consolation with the deep insight that "the greater the person, the greater his evil inclination."[500]

As a final note to this chapter, it should be mentioned that

Arizal as brought by Ben Ish Chai, *Rav Pealim, Sod Yishaarim* 10.

497. *Baba Matzia* 84a.
498. *Moreh Nevuchim* 1:32.
499. *Pesachim* 49b.
500. *Succah* 52a.

sin and its connection to the spiritual makeup of people is a complex subject. We have just seen that the women did not participate in the most grave sin of the Golden Calf, nor did they participate in the sin of the spies.[501] Nevertheless, the manifestations of sin are numerous. As an example, note the Maharal's commentary on Chazal's statement that the increase of wives leads to an increase of witchcraft. The Maharal says that good Jewish women most certainly do not engage in witchcraft; nevertheless some leaning toward that sin is more prevalent in women. This tendency results from a negative manifestation of a woman's spiritual leaning more toward the practical matters of Torah life. Accordingly a man is warned not to have many wives.[502] The Maharal's interpretation of Chazal's warning to men not to engage in excessive idle talk with women follows analogous logic.[503] Again, the entire subject of sin and its many causes and manifestations is quite complex and beyond the scope of this book.

---

501. *Midrash Rabbah* on *Bamidbar* 26:64.
502. Maharal, *Derech Chaim* 2:9.
503. Maharal, *Derech Chaim* 1:4. Cf. *Yeshuos Yaakov, Orach Chaim* 46:5. He explains that the blessing "made me according to His will" indicates that Hashem consulted the angels before creating man but not before creating woman. This consultation occurred because the creation of man has a greater effect on the angels, since is it is more probable for a man to sin and sins affect the angels. "According to His will" means according to Hashem's will alone and not that of the angels, who were not consulted for the woman's creation. It is not clear from the *Yeshuos Yaakov* whether the man's higher probability of sin is a function of an inborn inclination or whether it is the probable outcome of a man's assignment of a greater number of commandments. The more commandments one has, the more areas of life he has in

Fourteen

The Last Creation

A related popular myth stemming from the events of the creation is that the woman is higher than the man because she was
created after him. This myth is no doubt built off the principle
that the simplest creations happen first in the story of creation,
and the more spiritual and complex ones happen towards the end
of creation.[504] The biggest obstacle to this proposal is the verse
itself which says quite clearly, "Male and female He created
them."[505] As the Talmud and numerous later sources tell us, this
refers even to the physical creation of Adam as a composite of a
man and a woman.[506] In other words, the first man and woman

---

which to err. His higher probability of sin would be in proportion
to the extra duties incumbent on him. The higher probability may
be as well a function of the man's greater exposure to the outside
world and its temptations.

504. *Midrash Rabbah, Bereishis* 19:4; *Akeidas Yitzchok, shaar* 9;
Meam Loez, Bereishis 1:26.
505. *Bereishis* 1:27.
506. *Eruvin* 18a; *Moreh Nevuchim* 3:4; *Rashi* on *Bereishis* 1:27 quot-
ing the *Midrash Aggadah* as brought by *Eruvin* 18a; *Midrash
Haneelam Zohar Chadash* 16 as brought by *Torah Shelaimah*;
Meam Loez, Bereishis 2:21-22.

were created simultaneously. She was not created after him.

Rav Hirsch says that the simultaneous creation of the man and woman is evidenced in the grammar of the verses.

> God formed one side of Man into Woman; Man, as it were, was divided, and the one part formed into Woman, not *barah, yatzar, asa* but *banah,* only built out, arranged as Woman.[507]

The standard words for creation are not used by the formation of the woman. Hashem *vayiven* or built her. He did not *barah,* or create her, as in "*Elokim barah* the heavens and the earth"[508] and "Male and female He created [*barah*] them."[509] He did not *yitzar,* or form her, as in "And the Lord God formed [*vayitzar*] man of the dust of the ground."[510] He did not *asah,* or make her, as in "God made [*vaya'as*] the firmament"[511] and "Let us make [*na'aseh*] man in our image."[512] The woman had already been created.[513]

The Malbim offers analogous reasoning:

> For Adam and Chava were created attached as one, this next to this, the side of each in the other. And Hashem separated Chava and built her into a separate body fitting to be Adam's wife. Therefore the verse does not say "He made" or "He formed" since she was already made. It was [like one who] builds a building with

---

507. Rav Hirsch on *Bereishis* 2:21-22.
508. *Bereishis* 1:1.
509. *Bereishis* 2:22.
510. *Bereishis* 3:7.
511. *Bereishis* 1:7.
512. *Bereishis* 1:26.
513. See *Sefer HaCarmel, Otzar HaMalbim* for definitions of these words.

stones and the stones are already made.[514]

Again, Chava was created simultaneously with Adam, not afterwards. It may be mentioned as well the point of the Baal B'nei Yisaschar that the inner connection between husband and wife stems from their initial creation as one being.[515]

In partial contradistinction to the idea of purely simultaneous creation, the Maharal in *Gur Aryeh* seems to say that some aspects of the creation of Adam and Chava were not completed simultaneously. The Maharal says that the final creation of the man occurred last. While the formation of the woman followed that of the dual-gender being, the final formation of the man followed that of the woman. According to the Maharal, this is evidenced in the naming of the first being as Adam. Futhermore, the Maharal says that the man's later creation signifies that the man is at a higher spiritual level. The Maharal says that this sequence fits well with the differing ages at which boys and girls reach adult maturity. The Mishnah says that boys mature at thirteen and girls at twelve. In the words of the Maharal:

> You see throughout the [story of] creation that those [things] at a higher level came last. Therefore, the man came last....This is why the Rabbis say that the woman reaches maturity sooner than the man. The girl reaches it at twelve and a day and the boy at thirteen and a day, since this [his] is a great completion. The reason for this is that all things with more completeness, their completeness should come last. Therefore, the formation of the male is last and not first.[516]

The suggestion is that the construction of the male spiritual

---

514. Malbim on *Bereishis* 2:21-22. See also *Eruvin* 18a.
515. Baal B'nei Yisaschar, *Derech Pekudecha, Hakdamah* 9:4.
516. Maharal, *Gur Aryeh, Vayikra* 12, d'h *Ishah ki sazria.*

nature requires more preparation. Thus, the first male was created after the first female, and boys mature later than girls.

It should be mentioned that the earlier maturation of the female is a highly positive development in itself. As mentioned earlier, Rav Hirsch says that the Sages praise it and trace it to the woman's formation from the living being of Adam as opposed to that of earth which was the source of the physical part of Adam.[517] Again, the man and the woman each have different gifts to offer. One would not want both to develop at the same rate and in the same measure. In this author's view, the woman's earlier adult maturity would seem to give her a type of stability and sensibility. The boy's later development and higher spiritual ascension as an adult would seem to lend him energy and penetrating insight. Stability alone tends toward stagnation. Energy alone tends to self-destruction. The two qualities together offer the potential for real achievement. As a side note, this author has many times wondered, though he has not found a source to back it, that a woman's awesome ability to bear children might be a function of the source of her physical creation from a living being. Whatever its origins, this ability is obviously a fundamental and unique contribution to humanity.

In possible contrast to the Maharal, the *Yophe Toar* says that the principle of later creations being more spiritual applies to creations on separate days.[518] He comments on the Midrash which discusses the principle and lists examples of creations which differ in spirituality by virtue of their time of creation. The *Yophe Toar* notes that the Midrash does not draw any com-

---

517. Rav Hirsch on *Bereishis* 2:7. Rav Hirsch points out that the soul of Adam did not come from the earth, only the materials used to form him physically came from the earth.

518. The formation of the first woman occurred on the sixth day as did Adam's formation. The eating of the forbidden fruit by both of them occurred before Shabbos (*Meam Loez, Bereishis* 3:22).

parison between domesticated and undomesticated animals even though the domesticated animals were created after the undomesticated animals.

> The verse does not enumerate the domesticated and the undomesticated animal because the essential creation is determined by the day. Thus, even though ten things were created on the evening of Shabbos after the creation of Adam, these things do not have superiority over him.[519]

The ten creations of the evening of Shabbos can be found in *Pirkei Avos*. They include the gaping hole which swallowed Korach and his followers, the Well of Miriam which accompanied the generation of the desert, and the staff which Moshe used throughout the exodus from Egypt.[520] According to this Mishnah, some authorities say that demons too were created at this time. However, none of these take spiritual precedence over Adam and Chava, despite being created later than Adam and Chava, because all were created on the same day.

Interestingly, the *Akeidas Yitzchok* and the Abarbanel tell us that the subsequent formation of the woman is indicative of her role as helpmate to him.[521] In other words, man and woman were created simultaneously but formed independently to symbolize the nature of their relationship.

---

519. *Yophe Toar, Bereishis Rabbah* 19:4, *d'h VeAdam nivra* (Rav Shmuel Jaffe Ashkenazi, b. 16th century). The *Meam Loez* comments, "Israel is beloved by the Holy One, so in their merit the universe was created. And since they are the most beloved and precious of all, they were created on the last day" (*Meam Loez* 1:26).

520. *Pirkei Avos* 5:9 as explained by *The Hirsch Siddur, Pirkei Avos* 5:9, p. 493. Also appears in *Meam Loez, Bereishis* 1:27.

521. *Akeidas Yitzchok, Bereishis, shaar* 9; Abarbanel on *Bereishis* 2:18.

Fifteen

Avraham and Sarah

One of the most puzzling rationales for the popular statement that women are spiritually higher than men is built on a
Rashi, based apparently on a Midrash,[522] which discusses the
prophecy of Sarah. In *parashas Vayera*, Sarah expresses to
Avraham her fears about the pernicious influence of Hagar and
Ishmael on Avraham and Sarah's household.[523] For a variety of
reasons, which are much discussed in commentary on the
episode,[524] Avraham is reluctant to force Hagar and Ishmael out
of the house. However, Hashem speaks to Avraham and instructs
him: "Listen to Sarah in all that she tells you."[525] Rashi comments on the verse and says: "This teaches that Avraham was
secondary to Sarah in prophecy."[526]

Presumably, the leap from this Rashi to generalizations

---

522. *Midrash Rabbah, Shemos* 1:1. See *Midrash Rabbah, Bereishis*
    20:6 for apparent contradiction to the *Midrash* in *Shemos*. See
    also *Yophe Toar* and *Payrush Maharzav* on *Midrash Rabbah,
    Shemos* 20:6.
523. *Bereishis* 21:10.
524. See *Meam Loez, Bereishis* 21:11.
525. *Bereishis* 21:12.
526. *Rashi* on *Bereishis* 21:12.

about the spiritual natures of men and women is based on an assumption that prophecy is generally a reflection of spiritual development. Prophecy is said to require spiritual gifts and ethical development in accordance with the Torah.[527] There have been evil prophets such as Bilam whose prophecy was as developed as Moshe's. However, Bilam's prophecy emanated from negative forces[528] so it was achieved through an entirely different route than the righteous Sarah.

We are taught as well, however, that prophecy is a gift from Hashem depending on the needs of the time.[529] According to the *Akeidas Yitzchok*, Hashem may withhold prophecy from a deserving individual if the people of that person's generation do not deserve to have a prophet.[530] The *Akeidas Yitzchok* says as well that each prophet's environment affects his personality and his level of prophecy.[531] Rav Avigdor Miller connects this principle to the matter of Sarah's prophecy.

> She had been even greater than Avraham in prophecy *because she was able to avoid contact with the outside world*; [italics from Rav Miller]. Avraham, although her teacher, was somewhat hindered by the exigencies of practical life which may prevent prophecy at times (*Pesachim* 66b).[532]

So it would seem that prophecy and spiritual achievement are

---

527. *Mishneh Torah, Hilchos Yesodei Torah* 7:1; *Iyov* 28:25 as viewed by *Vayikra Rabbah* 15:2.
528. *Midrash Rabbah, Bamidbar* 20:6.
529. *Mishneh Torah, Hilchos Yesodei Torah* 7:5; *Moreh Nevuchim* 2:32.
530. *Akeidas Yitzchok, Shemos, shaar* 35.
531. *Akeidas Yitzchok, Shemos, shaar* 35.
532. Rav Avigdor Miller, *Behold A People* (Brooklyn: Balshin Printing and Offset Co. Brooklyn, NY., 5728), 68.

not directly correlated.

Even more so would prophecy and inborn spiritual endowment be only indirectly correlated. One has to ask why would Sarah's spiritual development necessarily reveal anything about her proclivities? Her development is her accomplishment. Why should one presume that she was born that way? Rashi's comment reflects Sarah's level after decades of dedication and struggle to divine service. His comment makes no reference to her innate qualities in comparison to those of Avraham.

Secondly, why assume Sarah's spiritual nature reveals anything about the rest of us. As the Talmud says, "A man differs from his friend in three ways: in voice, in appearance, and in understanding."[533] The Midrash says, "Just as no two faces are alike, no two people are alike."[534] This applies even to the *Avos* and *Imahos*. Avraham specialized in the trait of lovingkindness, Yitzchok in strict justice, and Yaakov in *emes*.[535] Each had is own personality. Why assume that all women are like Sarah? What about Rivka, Leah, and Rachel?

Moreover, why not sooner make the comparison to Adam and Chava? In their case, we at least have sources to say that the nature of their creation is reflective of the traits of everyday people.[536]

But even if one were to insist on attempting to compare the spiritual levels of Avraham and Sarah, he must refer to the Chidah who addresses the matter. The Chidah says that at one

---

533. *Sanhedrin* 38a.

534. *Midrash Tanchuma, Pinchas* 10.

535. Rav M. Miller, *Sabbath Shiurim* (Gateshead, England: Gateshead Foundation for Torah, 5730), p. 59.

536. *Tiferes Yisrael* 28; Rav Tzadok, *Dover Tzedek*, p. 127. As shown before, the Maharal says that Adam was more bonded with Hashem than was Chava (*Tiferes Yisrael* 28).

point Avraham and Sarah were equal in their *ma'alasam,* or
loosely translated "spiritual level," but later Avraham was at a
higher level. This change occurred at the hand of Hashem who
detracted from Sarah's level to enable the couple to have children. The Chidah cites a principle that a husband and wife at
equal levels cannot have children. After Hashem reduced
Sarah's level, the couple was able to procreate. The Chidah does
not explain the dynamics of this principle nor the exact meaning
of *ma'alasam.* This term is vague, and, as we have discussed,
spirituality has many components and functions. Nevertheless,
the words of the Chidah do serve as a meaningful contradiction
to the notion that Sarah was higher than Avraham.[537]

In addition to the Chidah's comments on the spiritual levels
of Avraham and Sarah and to the matter of the irrelevance of
connecting Rashi's point on Sarah's prophecy to generalizations
about men and women, there is the matter of how to interpret
Rashi in the first place. The Netziv comments as follows:

> There is to explain what is said that Avraham was sec-
> ondary to Sarah in prophecy. This is puzzling.
> Avraham was a great man who was spoken to by
> Hashem on numerous occasions. How could he be sec-
> ondary in prophecy to Sarah who was spoken to by
> Hashem one time [as depicted in the verse] "no, but
> you did laugh."[538] And the Midrash explains that it was
> Hashem speaking to her [in that verse].[539] Rather, the

---

537 Chidah, *Maris HaAyin, Berachos* 13.

538. *Bereishis* 18:15. Sarah had laughed upon hearing of the promise
      that she would bear children. Her laugh was an expression of
      doubt that such an event could happen in her advanced years. She
      was confronted for this lapse in faith, and after denying that she
      laughed was told, "no, but you did laugh."

539. *Midrash Rabbah, Bereishis* 48.

meaning was that Avraham was secondary to Sarah in divine inspiration [*ruach hakodesh*]. There are two types of communication with Hashem. Divine inspiration results when a person [on a high level] ponders and meditates intensely. Their resulting visions have a clear source, but this is not speech with Hashem. Prophecy is a greater level as we have explained [earlier]. David HaMelech, may he rest in peace, merited both of these. He said, "The spirit of Hashem spoke in me and filled my tongue." The "spirit of Hashem" refers to divine inspiration which appears by itself. "Filled my tongue" refers to actual prophecy. And Avraham was greater than Sarah in prophecy. However in divine inspiration, Sarah shined forth more than Avraham.[540]

In other words, the use of the word *navuah* or prophecy should not have been taken in the strict sense of the word. The high frequency of Avraham's prophecy in the Chumash should be the context in which we understand the comparison between Avraham and Sarah. The Midrash (or Rashi) was talking about a type of prophecy in a broadly defined sense of the word. Presumably, the Midrash assumed we would understand its words as such.

The Netziv explains the origins of these differing communications with the divine and why they would manifest differently in Avraham than they would in Sarah.

There are two reasons for this. Firstly, Avraham in his righteousness was leader of the world, directing it to the service of Hashem as it says, "Before us is the

---

540. *HaEmek Davar, Bereishis* 23:1 (Rav Naftali Tzvi Berlin, b. 19th century). See also Rashi on *Bereishis* 17:2.

prince of Hashem," a verse which shall be explained later. One who is involved with the masses is not free to ponder and meditate. Not so Sarah who dwelled in the tent in holiness and purity. Secondly, divine inspiration does not occur without peace of mind. Sarah, in her wondrous righteousness, was very strong in *emunah* [faith] and *bitachon* [trust]. As the Midrash explains, Sarah said to Avraham Avinu, "To you is the *bitachon*, to me the *emunah*." About the one who operates from the strength of *bitachon*, Chazal say, there is no real *bitachon* to the righteous in this world as sin may affect it. Sarah's *emunah* was not combined with promises so she did not have such worries, and she was set for divine inspiration.[541]

Both reasons are functions of Avraham's role as leader and *Godol HaDor*. The first reason should be clear. Avraham's responsibilites and exposure to the impurities of society were not conducive to the emotional state needed for divine inspiration. The second reason refers to explicit promises made to Avraham by Hashem concerning the future of the nation. As the *Meshech Chochmah* explains, promises for a blessing must come to fruition when prophesied to a group of people. However, promises made to an individual, that is, the prophet himself, are contingent on proper behavior by that individual. The promises made to Avraham concerning the inheritance of *Eretz Yisrael* were part of a covenant requiring extremely elevated behavior. Avraham, who was a giant in faith,[542] was confident

---

541. *HaEmek Davar, Bereishis* 23:1. See also *Yophe Toar, Midrash Rabbah, Shemos* 1:1 and *Yophe Toar* and *Payrush Maharzav, Midrash Rabbah, Shemos* 20:6.
542. *Akeidas Yitzchok, Bereishis, shaar* 26.

that his children would inherit the land as the promise for this inheritance came through a prophet (Avraham). However, Avraham worried about his inheritance since the prophecy was made directly to him.[543] It seems that this may be the emotional unrest referred to by the Netziv as being disruptive to the kind of peace of mind most conducive to *ruach hakodesh.*

In addition to this analysis of the Netziv, one must consider a Midrash in *Bereishis Rabbah* which says that Sarah's prophecy in general and that of the prophetesses was not as direct as that of prophets.[544] This Midrash may serve as well to show that the word "prophecy" used in the Midrash brought by Rashi should not be understood in the normal sense of the term.

None of this is even the slightest attempt to question the greatness of Sarah Emeinu. As the Netziv says, hers was a "wondrous righteousness." The Midrash tells us that Sarah was righteous throughout her life.[545] Rashi tells us that Sarah was at

---

543. *Meshech Chochmah, Bereishis* 15:8 (Rav Meir Simchah HaCohen, b. 19th century).

544. *Midrash Rabbah, Bereishis* 20:6. The Midrash says, "Rabbi Judah son of Rabbi Simon and Rabbi Yochanan in the name of Rabbi Eleazar son of Rabbi Simon said, 'The Holy One, blessed be He, never engaged to speak with a woman except that righteous one and even that was due to a particular circumstance.' Rav Abba son of Kahana said in the name of Rav Yitzchok, 'And what a roundabout way he spoke to her (as it is written), "And He said, 'No, but you did laugh.' " ' " (*Bereishis* 18:15) The Midrash goes on to give examples of divine communication to prophetesses coming through intermediaries such as angels. The *Yophe Toar* refers to a virtually identical Midrash (*Midrash Rabbah, Bereishis* 40:20) in his commentary on the Midrash in *Shemos Rabbah* which discusses the prophecy of Avraham and Sarah.

545. *Midrash Rabbah, Bereishis* 58:1 as brought by Malbim on *Bereishis* 23:1.

the age of 100 as free from sin as a girl who is not yet liable for sin.[546] Without her, there would be no Jewish people as Yitzchok, the next link in the spreading of the divine message to the world, could only be born with both Avraham and Sarah as his parents.[547] Rav Avigdor Miller says, "A considerable share of the holiness of this unique house (Avraham and Sarah's house) was owing to her presence. Her devotion to God and her eagerness in assisting Avraham in his endeavors for the truth and in the practice of hospitality and all kindliness *made her the model and prototype for all the righteous daughters of her people* [Italics from Rav Miller]."[548] Certainly, Sarah's greatness was beyond anything we can imagine.

Moreover, it is irrelevant to compare Sarah's spiritual stature to that of Avraham. Consider these following words of Rav Hirsch:

> We first note that throughout practically all the trials and sacrifices in which Abraham gave proof of his knowledge of God, his trust in God, his loyalty and obedience to God and his love of man, he was in close association with Sarah, and nearly all of them would have been impossible for him if Sarah had not been the faithful companion of his long wanderings, if Abraham's spirit had not filled Sarah also, and if she had not shared all his activities as his faithful comrade.[549]

Sarah, the righteous mother to us all, was Avraham's "faithful comrade," she was not his superior as such was not her role.

---

546. Rashi on *Bereishis* 23:1.
547. *Judaism Eternal*, vol. II, p. 62.
548. *Behold A People* 68.
549. *Judaism Eternal*, vol. II, p. 59.

Indeed, one must remember with whom we are dealing in Avraham Avinu. As the *Meom Loaz* says, the entire world was created in the merit of Avraham.[550] Coming from a family of idol worshippers and a world devoid of Torah, Avraham applied his extraordinary mind and spirit to perceive the unity and ruler-ship of Hashem.[551] He then courageously and single-handedly challenged and educated the world around him.[552] The Ramchal says that Avraham was the only person to elevate himself beyond the degraded level of man after the expulsion from the Garden of Eden. As a result, he was chosen by Hashem to found the Jewish nation and to lead the world out of its darkness.[553] The Midrash tells us that Hashem's communication with Avraham was the first such communication between Hashem and any person in ten generations. In the words of the Midrash, "The Almighty said, 'Of all the ten generations from Noach until you, I spoke to none but you.' Of all those generations He chose none other than him, and made a covenant not with them but with him alone."[554] The Mishnah says, "Five possessions the Holy One acquired for Himself in His world, and they are Torah, Heaven and Earth, Avraham, Israel, and the Holy Temple."[555] According to Rabbeinu Bachya, the merits of all the Jewish peo-ple are included in the merit of Avraham.[556] He is the foundation of everything we do. In the words of the Rambam, Avraham "is

---

550. *Meam Loez, Bereishis* 2:4 and 12:4.
551. *Mishneh Torah, Hilchos Avodas Cochavim* 1:3; *Akeidas Yitzchok, Bereishis, shaar* 16.
552. *Mishneh Torah, Hilchos Avodas Cochaivm* 1:3; *Akeidas Yitzchok, shaar* 16.
553. *Derech Hashem* 2:4:3.
554. *Midrash Rabbah, Bereishis* 39.
555. *Pirkei Avos* 6:10.
556. *Kad HaKemach, Halvanah.* (Rav Bachya ben Asher, b. 13th cen-tury).

the pillar of the world."[557] According to the *Akeidas Yitzchok*, the Torah describes Avraham as the role model par excellence of unselfishness and generosity.[558] The *Meom Loaz* says that Avraham's merit for the *Akeidah*, the binding of Yitzchok, is limitless. In times of trouble, we recite the chapter of the *Akeidah* and ask for Hashem's mercy on the merit of the *Akeidah*.[559] It is not likely that Sarah was his superior. One can almost imagine her horror at hearing such words. Rather, she was the perfect helpmate, his comrade, his *beshert*. It should be no coincidence that Rav Hirsch refers to Avraham's soaring spirit and Sarah's sense of propriety.[560] This is the epitome of a proper relationship between husband and wife.[561] And so Avraham mourned so heavily for Sarah at her passing.[562]

---

557. *Moreh Nevuchim* 3:29.
558. *Akeidas Yitzchok, Bereishis, shaar* 27.
559. *Meam Loez, Bereishis* 22:1. See also *Meam Loez, Bereishis* 12:8.
560. *Judaism Eternal,* vol. II, p. 63.
561. Rav Hirsch on *Bereishis* 12:8.
562. Rav Hirsch says: "We know what Sarah had been to Abraham, how infinitely deep his grief must have been. (Rav Hirsch on *Bereishis* 23:2); *Behold A People* #68.

Sixteen

The Redemption from Egypt

A similarly peculiar rationale for the popular statements concerning men's and women's spirituality stems from an idea of *Chazal* that the redemption from Egypt resulted from the merit of the righteous women. The statement was made in response to some heroic acts by the Jewish women in those times. The slavery of Egypt had worn down the spirit of the people. The men in their backbreaking work in the field expressed despair of the future and were reluctant to produce more children in those impossible times. But the women consoled their husbands, brought food to them in the fields, and encouraged them to build their families.[563] Upon these most meritorious acts of the women, Rabbi Akiva said, "In the reward of the righteous women, Israel was redeemed from Egypt."[564] The *Yophe Toar* explains that this refers to a speeding up of the redemption from its designated time of 400 years to 210 years.[565]

Much like the Rashi concerning Sarah's prophecy, this state-

563. *Meam Loaz, Shemos* 1:15.
564. *Midrash Rabbah, Shemos* 1:12. Also *Sotah* 11b and others listed in the *Mesuras HaMidrash* on *Midrash Rabbah, Shemos* 1:12.
565. *Yophe Toar, Midrash Rabbah, Shemos* 1:12.

ment about some specific acts by women in a special circumstance thousands of years ago has been taken by some people as information for comparisons of the spiritual levels of men and women. What's the connection? Even if one were to credit the Exodus exclusively to the merit of the women, which will be shown was not likely the case, why is that indicative of all history? Philosophical generalizations need more substantive grounding.

As for the cause of the redemption, one must consider a Gemara and a series of Midrashim which credit the redemption to other factors. The *Talmud Yerushalmi* says as follows:

> Because of five things was Israel redeemed from Egypt: [they are] the end [the predestined end of slavery], their distress, their cries, the merit of the fathers, and repentance.[566]

The *Midrash Rabbah* in *Shemos* offers a different list of causes:

> Because of four things Israel was redeemed from Egypt: They did not change their names and their language. They did not speak *lashon hara*. They did not involve themselves in immorality. And they did not change their family names.[567]

---

566. *Talmud Yerushalmi, Taanis* 1:1.
567. *Midrash Rabbah, Vayikra* 32:5. Also *Shir HaShirim Rabbah* 4 as brought by Maharal, *Netzach Yisrael, perek* 25, *d'h U'kshane*; The redemption as resulting from accomplishments of the entire nation can be found also in *Midrash Rabbah, Shemos* 1:28; *Tanchuma Balak* (brought in *Netzach Yisrael, perek* 25) and many others listed in the commentaries of the *Yophe Toar, Midrash Rabbah, Shemos* 1:28 and *Mesuras HaMidrash* and *Payrush Maharzav, Midrash Rabbah, Vayikra* 32:5.

A Midrash in *Shir HaShirim* presents the same list.[568] A Midrash in *Tanchumah Balak* mentions several of these achievements and mentions as well their not changing their style of clothing to that of the Egyptians.[569] A Midrash in *Pirkei d'Rebbi Eliezar* attributes a quickening of the redemption to the moaning of suffering Jewish children.[570] Rabbeinu Bachya says, "Israel was redeemed from Egypt only as a reward for faith, as it says, 'And the people believed.'[571] In the redemption to come, Israel will be redeemed as a reward for faith."[572]

So what was the cause of the speeding up of the redemption? Was it the merit of our righteous mothers for their support of their husbands and their families or was it the other righteous acts of the nation? The *Yophe Toar* asks this question and answers that "this and this caused" the redemption.[573] According to this explanation, the meaning of Rabbi Akiva's statement would seem to be that the merit of the righteous women was one factor among several in the redemption. It was not the only factor. The *Yophe Toar* lists as well numerous other Midrashim which credit a variety of factors in the redemption, including the merit of the *Avos* and *Imahos*, the merit of the tribe of Levi, and the merit of Yaakov Avinu. In view of these numerous Midrashim, the *Yophe Toar* offers a second explanation that perhaps these numerous views represent different opinions on the

---

568. See previous note.
569. See previous note.
570. *Pirkei d'Rebbi Eliezar* 48.
571. *Shemos* 4:31.
572. *Kad HaKemach, Emunah,* end. The *Pnei Moshe* interprets the *Talmud Yerushalmi (Taanis* 1:1) as attributing the coming redemption to the same five factors which the Talmud listed as causes of the redemption from Egypt.
573. *Yophe Toar, Midrash Rabbah, Shemos* 1:28.

matter. Either way, it seems quite a far stretch to take a single statement which conflicts with numerous other statements about a period in history and to draw from the statement philosophical generalizations about men and women.

Seventeen

The Midrash on the Influence of Wives

Much like the foregoing discussion on the sin of the Golden Calf, one can question philosophical generalizations that people sometimes draw from the Midrash about the influence of the good and evil wives. The Midrash speaks of a pious couple that had no children. Fearing Hashem's disapproval of the situation, the couple divorced, the husband marrying an evil woman and the wife marrying an evil man. In time, the good husband was turned evil and the evil husband was turned good. So, says the Midrash, this teaches that all is from the woman.[574]

No doubt, this is a powerful story meant to educate us. But what does it mean? It cannot mean that a wife determines whether her husband is evil or pious. The Talmud teaches, "All is in the hands of heaven except the fear of heaven."[575] This is a fundamental principle of the Torah. The Rambam explains:

All men have the choice whether to go toward the path of good and to be righteous or to go toward the path of

---

574. *Midrash Rabbah, Bereishis* 17:7.
575. *Berachos* 33b.

evil and be wicked. The choice is in his hands. Thus, it is written in the Torah, "Behold the man has become one of us, to know good from evil."[576] This is to say that man is unique in the world. There is no species comparable to him in this matter, that through his own knowledge and thought he can know good and evil, and he can do whatever he wants. No one prevents him from doing good or evil.[577]

Rav Hirsch explains the principle as follows:

God causes you to be born at such a time, at such a place, of such parents, in such an environment; He brings you into contact with such-and-such men, gives you such friends, such teachers, equips you with such faculties both of body and of mind, places you in such a position in life. He gives you all this as the means with which to carry out His will. Everything which falls to you you owe therefore directly to God, and again it is His will alone which you should fulfil with all that has fallen to your lot. 'Should,' not 'must'; for whether you will really fulfil it depends entirely on yourself. As the Sages say: 'Everything is in the hands of God except the fear of God'; everything is God's, only your heart is yours.[578]

Righteousness is in the hands of the individual. Furthermore, the Chumash says, "If you seek Him you will find Him."[579] David HaMelech tells us that "Hashem is near to all those that call

---

576. *Bereishis* 3:5.
577. *Mishneh Torah, Hilchos Tshuvah* 5:1.
578. *Horeb* 23.
579. *Devarim* 4:29.

upon Him,"[580] and "If you seek Him, He will be found."[581] The Gemara tells us, "If someone says, 'I labored but did not find' do not believe him. [If he says] 'I did not labor and I found' then do not believe him. [But if he says] 'I labored and I found' then believe him."[582] The Talmud tells us likewise of many cases of people who were immersed in impure surroundings but listened to their inner callings and strove for contact with the Almighty.[583]

The Midrash can likewise not be telling us that a wife should be a boss to her husband. Such would contradict an essential principle of the Torah as expressed in sources of every type and in every era. The Chumash tells us, "Your desire shall be for your husband, and he shall rule over you."[584] As shall be explained shortly, this is not a license for tyranny[585] but a call to the wife to focus on the husband and to encourage his leadership. The Midrash says that "a meritorious woman is one who does her husband's will."[586] The Gemara lists a man who is ruled by his wife as one of those whose life is not a life.[587] The Rambam says that a wife "should honor her husband exceedingly," "do all that he asks," and "should distance herself from all that he hates."[588] Rav Hirsch explains that the term "your

---

580. *Tehillim* 145:18.
581. *Divrei HaYamim* 1:28:9.
582. *Megillah* 6b.
583. *Avodah Zarah* 10b, 17a, and 18a; *Midrash Rabbah, Bereishis* 65:22.
584. *Bereishis* 3:16.
585. *Midrash Rabbah, Bereishis* 20:7.
586. *Tanna D'Bei Eliyahu* 9. A similar statement is made by the Malbim on *Bereishis* 2:18.
587. *Beitzah* 32b.
588. *Mishneh Torah, Hilchos Ishos,* 15:20.

desire" or *tashuasake* from the verse "your desire shall be for him" shows the extent of the wife's focus on the husband. This term is related to the word *shuk* which means leg or market. Just as all roads in a town lead to the market, the wife's whole being should be towards her husband. As Rav Hirsch says, her "whole effort shall be to please him, to win his love, to make him happy....."[589]

Some explanation of these verses on proper family structure may aid our discussion of the Midrash. Moreover, such explanation may be generally useful because of confusion about these matters in our times. Rav Hirsch says as follows:

> This will-subordination of the wife to the husband is a necessary condition of the unity which man and wife should form together. The subordination cannot be the other way about, since the man as *zachar*[590] has to carry forward the divine and human messages which through every marriage are to be a living force in the household, and to which the husband and wife are in union to devote their forces. Just as the first command of God though addressed to the man was given through him for the woman as well, just as in consequence Adam should not have thrown over the command of God for the sake of Eve but Eve ought to have subjected her desire to the will of God as expressed to her through Adam, so thenceforward the husband was to be responsible for the task imposed upon man by God and to carry it out in his marriage and household.[591]

Thus the parameters for the relationship between husband and

---

589. *Judaism Eternal*, vol. II, p. 58.
590. See chapter nine of this book.
591. *Judaism Eternal*, vol. II, p. 58.

wife are a direct function of the spiritual mission of the Jew in this world. Many sages have explained as well that it is in the nature of men and women to seek such a relationship.[592] This would follow from the concept that "the ways [of the Torah] are ways of pleasantness."[593] Our assignment is an enjoyable one.

In further explanation of this idea of respect for one's husband, it may help to propose that a chief function of the husband's position of leadership in the home is structure in the home. As Rav Yoel Schwartz explains:

> The "democratic ideal," say the experts, has made all former methods of education obsolete. A family hierarchy cannot succeed in a society where all are equal. In the past, the father's will was respected by wife and child. With the advent of "equality" and now also, Women's "Lib," he has lost his position in the home in relation to his wife, and as a result both he and his wife have lost their authority over their children.[594]

Thus, the home itself needs the traditional family structure. Incidentally, it is implied here that the husband need not possess perfect insight and judgment to assume his position as head of the family. The family needs structure, and the man for a variety of reasons, including perhaps his typical possession of a mind and personality most conducive to leadership,[595] assumes the general role of leader.[596]

---

592. See, for example, *Midrash Rabbah, Bereishis* 20:7.
593. *Mishlei* 3:17.
594. Rav Yoel Schwartz, *The Eternal Jewish Home* (Jerusalem: Jerusalem Academy Publications, 1982), pp. 20-21. (trans. by Yona Bernstein) (Rav Yoel Schwartz, contemporary).
595. See *Megillah* 14a.
596. Rav Avigdor Miller, personal communication with author.

As a note on the foregoing point, the author would like to suggest an idea that the giving of respect (and love as well) are as much a need of the giver as of the recipient. It is not merely that respect for the head of the household benefits the household. Rather, it benefits the one who acts respectfully. In other words, a husband can feel and show love and respect for his wife even though she is not the perfect "woman of valor." Similarly, a wife can feel and demonstrate respect and love for her husband even though he is not a leading scholar and a perfect saint. Such an idea may be suggested in the following Midrash:

> There is a story of a woman from the house of Tiberia who was married to a bandit. He caused her much distress. The Rabbis heard of this situation and came to reprimand the man. When [the woman] came before the Rabbis, she held before them a menorah of gold with a clay lamp on top of it. This fulfills what is said "and to your husband will be your desire."[597, 598]

In this instance, the wife was performing her job far better than the husband was performing his. Nevertheless, the wife saw it best to maintain a traditional relationship. She continued to focus on her husband as a candlestick does to a candle even though her actions were of golden quality and his of clay. The showing of respect is rewarding in itself.

It should be likewise added that a home, or any social structure, cannot function with two leaders. Of course, the home can have and should have two sources of inspiration and insight, but it cannot have two final authorities just as a car cannot have two drivers. This idea is well expressed by the Midrash where

---

597. *Bereishis* 3:16.
598. *Midrash Rabbah, Bereishis* 20:7.

Eliyahu HaNavi visits a town of people who were not behaving properly and blesses them to have many leaders. Rebbe Yehoshua ben Levi, who had accompanied Eliyahu HaNavi on the trip, expressed surprise at this blessing and the blessing given earlier to a town of good people that they should have one leader. Eliyahu HaNavi explained that it was incumbent on him to decree destruction to the town of evil people so he blessed them with many leaders. As he explained further, a place with many leaders will self-destruct. In the place where the people conducted themselves properly, he hoped for them to have one leader. A place with one leader will ultimately endure.[599] *Chaim shel Osher*[600] connects to this topic the Gemara concerning the two great lights. Originally, the sun and the moon shone with equal brightness. The moon asked Hashem, "How can two kings rule in one kingdom?" Hashem responded, "Therefore you should make yourself smaller."[601] According to *Chaim shel Osher,* the Sages teach us that since ultimately the moon acted humbly by making itself smaller, Hashem gave it a guarantee of future compensation.[602]

It should be worth digressing further to point out a husband's obligation to treat his wife with love, consideration, and respect. The Chumash outlines a husband's responsibilities concerning physical sustenance[603] and intimacy[604] and calls on him

---

599. Brought by *Chaim shel Osher*, vol. II, p. 52.
600. *Chaim shel Osher*, vol. II, p. 52.
601. *Chulin* 60b.
602. *Midrash Rabbah, Bereishis* 6:3-4.
603. *Shemos* 21:10. See also *Pesachim* 109a.
604. *Shemos* 21:10; Rambam, *Hilchos Ishos* 12:2; *Shulchan Aruch, Even HaEzer* 69:2. See also *Chasam Sofer* to *Kesuvos* 70a who says that the husband's financial support of the wife must be done in a pleasant and cheerful manner.

to set a proper tone by being especially concerend with his wife's happiness in the first year of marriage.[605] The Gemara says that a man should love his wife as himself and should honor her more than himself.[606] He is told that the blessings on the home will not come if he does not treat her properly.[607] The Rambam says that he should speak to her in a warm manner, and he should not appear depressed around her.[608] In addition, the numerous prescriptions in the Torah for righteous treatment of others apply to marriage. Each of us is told to "love your neighbor as yourself,"[609] and to "walk in His ways,"[610] meaning those of Hashem Who is compassionate and just.[611] We are told not to "hurt another with words"[612] or to "have a strange God within you,"[613] which the Sages say can be taken as a reference to anger.[614] Our righteous leaders have been role models in sensitive and humane conduct towards others. The Talmud says "Be like the students of Aaron, loving peace and pursuing peace"[615] and "A man should always be patient like Hillel."[616]

Furthermore, the husband's leadership of the home must necessarily be conducted as an expression of Torah principles. He is responsible to humble, discipline, and develop himself in

---

605. *Devarim* 25:5; *Sefer HaChinuch* 549.
606. *Yevamos* 62b. See also *Mishneh Torah, Hilchos Ishos,* 16:12.
607. *Baba Matzia* 59a.
608. *Mishneh Torah, Hilchos Ishos* 15:19.
609. *Vayikra* 19:18.
610. *Devarim* 28:9.
611. *Sefer HaMitzvos HaKatzar, M'A* 9.
612. *Vayikra* 25:17.
613. *Tehillim* 81.
614. *Shabbos* 105b.
615. *Pirkei Avos* 1:12.
616. *Shabbos* 30b.

accordance with Hashem's commandments and the teachings of the Rabbis. As the Mishnah says, "Be exceedingly humble,"[617] "let the awe of Heaven be upon you,"[618] "nullify your will before His will,"[619] and "let your house be a meeting place for the wise men. Sit amongst the dust of their feet, and drink their words thirstily."[620]

Of course, the principle of general spiritual leadership by the husband should not obscure the potential benefit of the wife's input into family concerns. As mentioned before, the Gemara says that regarding practical matters of the household, the husband should take his wife's counsel.[621] We see as well in our history occasions where initiative and input by wives helped prevent tragic occurrences. A classic example is the sin of the Golden Calf where the women refused to contribute their jewelry towards the making of the calf.[622] Another example is Rivka and the blessings of Yaakov and Eisav.[623] Rivka knew through divine inspiration that Eisav was not worthy of the blessings. Yitzchok's reasons for insisting on blessing Eisav are a complex subject; nevertheless the blessings had to go to Yaakov. In the end, Rivka resorted to indirect means to bring her husband to bless Yaakov.[624] *Chaim shel Osher*, in addressing these cases, tells us that such opposition to one's husband should come only when prohibitions or dangers are "clear without any shadow of doubt."[625] He adds that "practically speaking, without asking a

---

617. *Pirkei Avos* 4:4.
618. *Pirkei Avos* 1:3.
619. *Pirkei Avos* 2:4.
620. *Pirkei Avos* 1:4.
621. *Baba Matzia* 59a.
622. *Meom Loaz, Shemos* 32:3.
623. *Bereishis* 27.
624. *Bereishis* 27.
625. *Chaim shel Osher,* vol. II, p. 244.

qualified advisor, a woman will usually not know if it is proper for her to use this method."[626] He says as well that the obligation to speak in a pleasant manner applies even in situations involving clear sins.[627] Furthermore, says *Chaim shel Osher*, in situations not of clear halachic danger but of the wife's personal preferences or objections, she should not try to compel her husband. Rather, she may mention her idea in a delicate manner which leaves him with the decision.[628]

This distinction in the nature of the wife's input is due to the dual quality of her influence on her husband. The women refused participation in the sin of the Golden Calf. In that case, where the sinfulness of the deed was clear, the input by the wives was most constructive. Alternatively, Chava persuaded Adam to eat from the forbidden fruit. In that case, the motivation was desire, including apparently, a desire to attempt a novel path of spiritual growth.[629] The result, of course, was most destructive. Death was brought into the world.[630]

The author would feel remiss if he did not mention that these comments concerning the conduct of husbands and wives portray ideals whose realistic attainment is an entire subject in itself. One can imagine that these verses should not be used as gauges by which to find displeasure with one's spouse. Each of us should endeavor to grow in our level of conduct towards other people, and, it would seem, that part of that growth is a focus on one's own level of conduct and not on that of his or her partner. The *Baalei Mussar* frequently point out that each person should be concerned with his own *ruchnius* or spiritual responsi-

---

626. *Chaim shel Osher,* vol. II, p. 244.
627. *Chaim shel Osher,* vol. II, p. 244.
628. *Chaim shel Osher,* vol. II, p. 245.
629. *Akeidas Yitzchok, Bereishis, shaar* 9.
630. *Talmud Yerushalmi, Shabbos* 2:6.

bilities and his companion's *goshmius* or physical needs. The verses regarding behavior toward one's fellow should be motivation for our personal growth not our personal demands.

Furthermore, the pursuit of these ideals should no doubt be attempted with dignity and common sense. Just as no person is entitled to be a tyrant, no person should allow him or herself to be trampled upon and treated without dignity. On this point, it should be said that the general approach of this book is that of examining general philosophical outlooks; it is not a guide for dealing with specific practical situations. The author would like to stress that while it is important for one to cultivate proper philosophical outlooks, it is important also to know the difference between philosophy and practicality. As a note, the book *Fulfillment in Marriage* contains a number of useful chapters on the practical handling of difficult marital situations. These include problems caused by negligent or abusive spouses.

It should be pointed out as well that domination of others by any person is not in the spirit of the Torah. A prime example of this is Moshe's reluctance to assume the role as leader of the nation even though Hashem Himself had appointed Moshe for the role.[631] Moshe expressed such stringent hesitations that Hashem finally had to reprimand him to take the position.[632] The Gemara tells us that Yoseph HaTzadick died earlier than did his brothers because of his assumption of the posture of authority.[633] The reality is that Hashem is in command of all of us. As we say every time we make a blessing, Hashem is "King of the universe." In our prayers we say, "The kingship and the rulership belong to the God of the worlds."[634] In Tanach we find the

---

631. *Shemos* 4:13; *Akeidas Yitzchok, Shemos, shaar* 35.
632. *Shemos* 4:14; *Akeidas Yitachok, Shemos, shaar* 35.
633. *Berachos* 55a; *Sotah* 13b.
634. *Tefillas HaAderes VeHaEmunah.*

verse "To you Hashem is the kingdom and the supremacy over all."[635] This fact should be integrated into our personalities so that no person strives to rule gratuitously over other people. Moshe did accept the role of leader of the Jewish people, but he did so out of Hashem's command and because the people needed him to be their leader.[636]

Getting back to the Midrash, one must say also that the Midrash cannot be calling for the wife to offer overt spiritual leadership in the home. The *Sefer Chasidim*,[637] in an apparent commentary on this Midrash, refers to a Gemara which contradicts such an idea:

> Rav says the one who goes about in the counsel of his wife ends up in *Gehenom*, as it says, "But there was none like Ahab, who sold himself to doing what was evil in the sight of the Lord at the instigation of his wife Jezebel."[638] Rav Pappa said to Abaye, "But [don't] people say 'If your wife is short, bend down so that you can hear her counsel?' " This is no difficulty; one statement refers to matters of the world and one refers to matters of the house. Another interpretation; one refers to matters of heaven and one refers to matters of the world.[639]

In other words, the wife is not supposed to be the overt spiritual leader of the house. The *Sefer Chasidim* adds that this Gemara applies even if the wife is a *yiras shemayim*, or fearer of Heaven. As Rav Hirsch has explained, spiritual leadership of the home is

---

635. *Devrei HaYamim* 1:29:11.
636. *Midrash Rabbah, Shemos* 3:4-5.
637. *Sefer Chasidim* 135.
638. *Melachim* I, 21:25.
639. *Baba Matzia* 59a.

the husband's responsibility.[640] Of course, the wife can inspire her family with her actions and help in the guidance of the family through her expression of wisdom. Furthermore, as the latter piece of this Gemara explains, in matters of the household, such as feeding and clothing the children in the sense that they are not spiritual issues, the husband should listen to the counsel of his wife.[641]

Interestingly, the Maharal uses this Gemara to explain the statement of Chazal that "the woman is given extra understanding or *binah yaseirah*."[642] He says that the woman has a *seichel elyoni* a phrase which loosely translated means "an ethereal [or less concrete] intelligence." The man's *seichel hanivdal,* or, loosely translated, "abstract intelligence" works better to sort out spiritual matters.[643] As others have explained, the man's intelligence, which tends to work in a more organized and detailed fashion, also lends itself better to scrutiny.[644] It is therefore safer to have the man as the final authority in decisions of a spiritual nature. The woman may certainly offer deep and useful philosophical insights but her form of intelligence, which works hand in hand with her emotional nature, makes it difficult for her to check the objectivity of her conclusions. However, these same qualities which make objectivity more difficult to achieve are ideal attributes for the building of a Jewish home. This challenging and invaluable task requires numerous qualities including

---

640. Rav Hirsch on *Bereishis* 12:8.
641. As interpreted by *Mitzvos HaBayis* 8:5.
642. *Niddah* 45b.
643. Maharal, *Chidushei Agaddos, Baba Matzia* 59a.
644. Rav Tuvia Yehuda Tuviomi from *Bais Yisrael: HaMishpacha HaYahudis,* collected by Yechezchiel Rotenberg (B'nei Brak: Nezach, 1981), pt. 1, pp. 38-40; Rav Nachman Bullman, personal communication with author.

intuitive insight into human relations, wisdom into the nature of life, practical intelligence and ingenuity, and personal warmth.

Rav Hirsch sees in the story of Avraham and Sarah a model for proper division of responsibility in the home. He comments on a verse in *Lech Lecha* in which Avraham tells his family to move their encampment to a different location. Rav Hirsch points out that while the grammatical gender of the verb *vayataik* depicting Avraham's command is in the masculine, the word for tent or *ohelah* is in the feminine.

> It is significant that it says *ohelah*, written with the feminine *hei*, as opposed to *vayataik*. Whereas there, where it affected the whole household, Avraham had to exert his authority, *vayataik*, possibly even to persuade Sarah, here in the home, his house was really Sarah's house. For external matters the man, internal ones the woman; as leader; guiding star , to submit the whole household in every way to the Will of God, the man is in authority, in every other matter of managing and directing the home, the woman has precedence. Such is the principle of intimate happy Jewish life, the origin of which has its roots in Avraham's tent.[645]

Again one sees the important and multifaceted role of the woman in managing the home. One sees also that overt spiritual leadership of the home is the husband's domain.

Given all of these comments of our Sages, one wonders what is the meaning of our Midrash? The wife does not determine the religiousness of her husband. She does not, Heaven forbid, dominate her husband. She does not offer overt religious leadership over her husband. So what is the meaning of the phrase "all is from the woman"?

---

645. Rav Hirsch on *Bereishis* 12:8.

The *Payrush Maharzav* connects the phrase to the description of the first woman's formation from the side of Adam. The woman was taken from the man. As the verse says, "From the man this was taken."[646] Accordingly, says the *Payrush Maharzav*, the "heart and mind" of the man go after the woman.[647]

It would seem from the words of the *Payrush Maharzav* the man has an emotional attraction to the woman as one usually does to something that belongs to him or is a part of him. Accordingly, one could hypothesize that the influence of the woman results from her emotional qualities. Perhaps the Midrash uses such strong language to force the man to see what he might otherwise overlook given the man's nature and responsibilities. These responsibilities, particularly that of earning a living, may preclude the development of certain types of emotions. Perhaps the Midrash also serves to help a woman to see what she might overlook because of her immersion in emotional life. The emotional orientation of a woman was discussed earlier. The Chumash offers several episodes where woman displayed keen emotional insight.[648] The Gemara speaks of the connection many women have had to prayer[649] and also speaks of a woman's compassion[650] and a woman's tears.[651] These come from emotional traits which may cause an unexpected influence on a man — for better or worse.

Ohel Rachel also interprets the Midrash as indicating the

---

646. *Bereishis* 2:23.
647. *Payrush Maharzav, Midrash Rabbah, Bereishis* 17:4.
648. *Bereishis* 21:10 and 27:5-16.
649. *Berachos* 31a and 31b; *Taanis* 23b; *Berachos* 7b.
650. *Megillah* 14b.
651. *Sotah* 17a; *Baba Matzia* 59. Also in *Judaism Eternal*, vol. II, p. 95.

emotional influence of a wife on a husband. It quotes the Midrash which attributes Chava's influence on Adam to her crying to him. As the Midrash says, "Not by her asking was it done but by her crying."[652] *Ohel Rachel* then discusses various emotional traits of women and the value of these qualities on home life. These qualities, such as her yearning for her husband and her desire to make a home, can serve as catalysts to a man's endeavors.[653] The implication seems to be that many men simply continue in the direction at which they first began their activities as catalyzed by their wive's emotions. On this point, this author has heard from a number of scholars that this Midrash speaks to the occasion where the husband is not particularly driven from his own internal motivations. In a situation where the husband has a strong sense of purpose, the wife's influence does not normally determine his direction.

---

652. *Midrash Rabbah, Devarim* 4:5.
653. *Ohel Rachel*, by the author of *Mishkan Rachel* (Jerusalem: Ruchamah Graphikut, 5742), *haskamahs* by Rav Shlomo Wolbe and Rav Moshe Halberstam. *Mishkan Rachel* has *haskamahs* by Rav Shlomo Eliyashiv, Rav Y. Weiss, and Rav Nissim Karelitz.

Eighteen

Ramifications of the Misconceptions

The teaching of oversimplified or false principles concerning the spiritual natures of men and women produces a number of negative repercussions. This should be no surprise. Just as proper teachings uplift us, improper teachings cause us to stumble. Since misteachings on this subject are a relatively recent occurrence, the classical commentaries have not focused on them. Accordingly, the analysis offered here is more exclusively that of the author of this book. He shall endeavor to base his comments on that of the classic sources, but the application of the sources will be the work of this author.

One of the problems with apologetic teachings is their hindrance to outreach to non-religious Jews. While the intent of many popular teachings on these subjects is to achieve success in outreach, the ironic result is a pushing away of many individuals who sense their distortion. Many estranged Jews come to Torah in their frustration with dishonesty in society. The world today is awash in commercialism and pecuniary ambition. It is an environment which encourages deceit as the barrage of scandals in business and politics so potently demonstrates. Obviously, the world is home as well to honest people, but a few good souls do not make secular culture adequate source material for a person's life outlook. Secularized Jews come to Torah life in large part to experience integrity and honesty. Purposely manipulating the Torah is self-defeating in addition to being forbidden as previously explained. People can sense the deceit, and sooner or later the resentment emerges. As the Sages tell us, words spoken sincerely from the heart will enter the heart of the listener.[654] Words spoken not necessarily even with conscious manipulation, but spoken without proper research as to their truth cannot be spoken with sincerity. One can sense the dubiousness of his own position. Accordingly, his attempts at outreach are undermined.

Additionally, some people may resent the implied condescension and patronizing of apologetic teachings. It would seem that one assumption behind the dissemination of apologetics is a low estimation of a student's ability to appreciate the truth. Certainly, the Torah's depiction of the roles and natures of men and women can be challenging to grasp at first; particularly for those of us relatively more immersed in secular culture. However, apologetic teachings in their perversion of the dictates of common sense can be insulting. They carry with them an implied chauvinism that not only are women unable to appreciate the truth but will accept an untruth clearly designed to win the favor of an audience. Accordingly, such teachings are simultaneously complementary and insulting. They deliver a mixed message that can be most unsettling. Perhaps a greater faith in the commitment and intelligence of Jewish women would suggest the ability of Jewish women to perceive the fairness and wisdom of unadulterated Torah views on these subjects.

A second problem for outreach is that fact that these teach-

---

654. Rav Eliyahu Lopian, *Lev Eliyahu,* vol. I, p. 169.

ings dissuade many men from becoming Torah observant. One has to wonder sometimes if people even think about that. Is a young man who has been out in the world really supposed to believe that he is less naturally moral and good than his female peers? Does not such a teaching mirror the reverse gender discrimination and "male bashing" that he endures in the secular world? In his journies, he has met good men and good women, bad men and bad women, and now he is told that really women are better? Mind you, women should not be told that men are better as this is not the case either. Rather, each gender has its strengths and its occasions to shine, as hopefully has been explained. It is a more complex and balanced picture than the idea that one is categorically better.

As one may imagine, the road to Torah observance may be difficult at first for people who were raised in secular environments. We may be familiar with the challenges of young women who have had to contend with many issues including their past training in gender roles. Young men face many challenges as well including the overcoming of increasingly popular secular teachings which encourage men to view themselves and their roles in ways which conflict with the responsibilities of a Jewish man. This was touched upon earlier. The lives of Jewish men and women can both seem discriminatory. Of course, both roles are in reality the most liberating experiences available to people, but sometimes the reality is not initially apparent. Numerous men have asked, Why do I have to get up early when she does not? Why am I the only one responsible for supporting the family? This person is hardly appeased when he overhears someone saying that his responsibilities stem from deficiencies in his spiritual makeup. Such an outlook is not particularly motivating (besides being false). In fact, such an attitude can serve as a "turn-off," Heaven forbid.

Remember also that men face the additional challenge of coming to appreciate the prioritizing of Torah learning over career development. Career aspirations have been for many of these men the chief focus of their lives. Many women also have worked many years on their careers, but this is not as common with women in general. Additionally, many of these men were top students who now find themselves as ignorant in Torah study as children. They enter a world that values neither their secular education nor their career success. It is by no means an easy transition for many men just as it is not for many women. Needless to say, the souls of Jewish men and Jewish women are both invaluable and neither should be appealed to in a way which pushes away the other.

Additionally, one could argue that the entire strategy of portraying women as spirituality more advanced than men displays an ignorance about women. If one takes the time to analyze the apologetic teachings, he or she might find in them a distinctively unfeminine quality. A contest of superiority is not a particularly feminine enterprise. One sees such an interest increasingly in our mixed up world, but deep down it is not what most women seek. Indeed, we see in the dating world that just about all women seek a man they can look up to. She wants him to be taller, smarter, and richer. The Gemara advises men to be aware of this principle when they prepare for marriage.[655] Why in the most important area of life--spirituality--would a woman want to find that men are inferior? One can imagine the implications of such teachings in the dating world. Whom can a woman marry now?

Thus, not only is it incorrect to say that the woman is spiritually higher than the man, but it is irrelevant. It seems to miss the whole essence and specialness of femininity. An addressing

---

655. *Yevamos* 63a as explained by *Chaim shel Osher*, vol. I, p. 237.

of this ramification of apologetic teachings is one of the primary motivations of this book. The classical sources presented in these last few chapters have not been brought to take anything away from women, but rather to give something back to them. To apply a metaphor, it is futile for a deer to attempt to fly like a dove just as it is for a dove to attempt to bound through the forest like a deer. We work best and grow best in accordance with our natures. The Talmud tells us that the "hard service" of Egypt consisted of women doing men's work and men doing women's work.[656] We can imagine that the enslavement of our current exile also consists in part from a confusion of roles and from an accompanying confusion of identities as well. The apologetic teachings on the spiritual natures of women give a distorted picture of Jewish life and may leave many women feeling more lost than found in the long run, Heaven forbid.

In addition to the ultimate perniciousness of apologetic teachings, one must consider the simple ineffectiveness of apologetics in the short run. These teachings do not affect an interest in Judaism nearly as much as some people seem to believe. As mentioned, many women are turned off by the insincerity, dubiousness, and irrelevancy of the apologetics. Rather, deep down most women seek love and appreciation. It should be no surprise that the Sages offer numerous statements to convey how a husband should value and love his wife. Many women seek as well a life experience of emotional connection and personal creativity, both of which are not addressed at all by apologetic teachings.

And what about the implications in marital relationship? One woman described the problem to the author as follows:

When women bandy around this idea about women

---

656. *Sotah* 11b.

being more spiritual, it ends up spilling over into relationships with men. It becomes big. It becomes like a monster because it feeds on their insecurities. Women are very insecure. They don't know who they are, and they use this. They are getting reassurance from something that is not true. They are saying, "well I'm going to feel good about myself by saying I'm more spiritual." Well that sets up an adversarial relationship. In that "I'm more spiritual than you." And so she's going to see her husband in a different way. As opposed to when she tries to deal with who she is as a woman. That helps her to see herself differently or to clarify who she is as a woman. And that helps her to see her husband for who he is rather than compare or make herself better than he is.

The apologetic teachings disrupt as well the religious atmosphere in the home. The Talmud tells us that the man should be the spiritual leader in the home.[657] Who would accept the leadership of an inferior? Young women can be taught day in and day out to respect the leadership of their husbands, but if they are taught simultaneously to doubt the qualifications of the leader, then the teachings are undermined. So, say some, the learning equips the husbands. This works fine for the learned Rabbi. What about a regular guy? What if he is not so learned? At what point is the learning considered adequate to lift him to a position of authority? Who decides? As a different woman phrased it, "If women are more spiritual, then we should be the rabbis."

Part of the problem in this regard is confusion over the meaning of the term *binah yaseirah*, or extra intuition. This is a personality attribute which is widely associated with the female

---

657. *Baba Matzia* 59a.

nature and often exaggerated as to its nature and application. The Mishnah in *Niddah* discusses the age at which young boys and girls can be considered responsible for their vows, in other words, their age of maturity. Rebbe says that girls reach maturity at age twelve and boys at thirteen, Rabbi Shimon ben Eliezar says that boys reach maturity at twelve and girls and thirteen.[658] The Gemara's explanation for the view of Rebbe Shimon is that boys develop their practical intelligence through their exposure to the marketplace. The explanation for the view of Rebbe is that girls have *binah yaseirah* which is intuition that, depending on different opinions, may mean extra intuition or earlier developing intuition.[659]

The definition of this extra intuition has been discussed in this book. The Maharal calls it a *seichel elyoni*, or loosely translated, ethereal or non-concrete intelligence. The full text of the Maharal's comments appear as follows:

> The explanation is that Hashem gave to the woman an ethereal intelligence since she is extra prepared for this. To the man He gave intelligence and wisdom [*chochmah*] in extra amounts, and this is an abstract intelligence. Accordingly, it says in *Perek Hazahav* (Baba Metzia 59a in the Gemara). "If your wife is short, bend down and listen to her." It is established that this refers to matters of the house or according to another interpretation matters of the world. This is so because the woman's wisdom comes from ethereal intelligence which is more relevant to her than it is to the man. Therefore it says that in matters of heaven that one should not go after the counsel of his wife.

---

658. *Nidah* 5:6. See also *Midrash Rabbah Bereishis* 18:1.
659. *Nidah* 45b.

Because wisdom required for such matters is not relevant to her, it being an abstract intelligence. There is to understand well what our Rabbis hint at when they say that [Hashem] gave *binah yaseirah* [to the woman]. This is drawn from the language *vayiven* [a reference to the verse where Hashem builds or *vayiven* the woman from the side of the man]. She completes the building of the man and from this perspective wisdom is relevant to her. Nevertheless, the attribute of the man is that he has abstract intelligence.[660]

There is much going on in this passage, but what should be clear is that the intuition of a woman corresponds to her role as helpmate and mother. The reference to her completing the building of the man seems to refer to her contributions as helpmate. As the Maharal explains in his commentary on *Pirkei Avos*, the man needs the woman to keep his home.[661] Rav Hirsch details the vital spiritual, intellectual, and, emotional components of a woman's responsibilities in the home.[662] Therefore, just as a woman is made to be a helpmate, it would seem that her intelligence is especially equipped for her being a helpmate.

The problem is that people sometimes misunderstand the meaning of *binah yaseirah* and take it effectively to refer to some comprehensive link to truth. Such a practice might be reflective of the trend in the secular world towards religions from the Far East, which operate with little literature and focus on meditation and internal wisdom. Of course, Judaism recognizes the value of internal messages but considers them useless and even dangerous without the discipline of Torah to refine our instincts and to tell us right from wrong. Many times our hunch-

---

660. Maharal, *Chidushei Agados, Nidah* 45b.
661. *Derech Chaim* 2:8.
662. *Judaism Eternal*, vol. II, chapter two.

es reflect more imagination than insight. This happens of course to both men and women.

Further refining the matter is that fact that many commentators view *binah yaseirah* not as extra intuition, but as earlier occurring intuition. The *Midrash Aggadah* explains that girls develop *binah* earlier, but when boys go out into the marketplace they develop it to an even higher level.

> "And [Hashem] built," this teaches that the Holy One gave *binah* to the female more than to the male. However, when the male goes to the outside world, he learns *binah* from the people there. Therefore, the man after maturation understands better than does the woman.[663]

The *Tosfos HaRosh* says that this is the explanation of Rebbe's words in the Gemara in *Nidah* as brought earlier here.[664] The matter may be complicated in our times by the fact that boys and girls both have significant exposure to the marketplace.

It appears that Rashi also may view *binah yaseirah* as earlier occurring intuition.[665] That is to say, girls develop it sufficiently for maturity at twelve and boys at thirteen. Rashi explains that girls are more free to develop *binah,* since their strength is not drained from the study of Torah.[666] In the author's view, this does not necessarily contradict the words of the Maharal who seems to describe *binah* as a more naturally occurring trait. Perhaps the slightly later development by the boys occurs through the more traditionally masculine path of logical devel-

---

663. *Midrash Aggadah, Bereishis* 2:24:16. Also in *Torah Shelaimah, Bereishis*, notes to 284.
664. *Tosfos HaRosh, Nidah* 45b.
665. *Torah Shelaimah, Bereishis*, notes to 284.
666. *Rashi* on *Kasuvos* 3a.

opment. Accordingly, a boy's acquisition of extra *binah*, as referred to in the *Midrash Aggadah* and the *Tosfos HaRosh*, may not be *binah* in its every manifestation. The more ethereally based *binah* of a woman may still retain advantages in some regards. Either way, *binah* is not *navuah* and must not be taken as a secret channel to truth. It is an important type of intelligence but must be checked by Torah and *chochmah* just as *chochmah* must be supplemented by *binah*. As the Mishnah says, "Where there is no wisdom, there is no fear [of Heaven]. Where there is no fear [of Heaven] there is no wisdom. Where there is no understanding, there is no knowledge. Where there is no knowledge, there is no understanding."[667]

Further complicating the subject is the Rambam who states that the checking of vows at earlier ages by girls occurs because the life expectancy of women in previous generations was shorter than that of men.[668] This is not the place to analyze this source, but it is brought to give a sense of the complexity of this subject and the care one must take in handling it.

Returning to the discussion of ramifications of improper teachings, there remains to be discussed the most serious ramification of *bitul Torah*, or wasted opportunity for Torah study. As explained numerous times throughout this book, the commandment of *Limud Torah* is considered the greatest commandment of all and the producer of the greatest reward for those who perform it. As the Midrash says, "Great is the Torah for it gives life in this world and in the world to come, as the verse says, 'For they [the words of Torah] are life to those who find them and, they heal his flesh.' "[669] [670] The Midrash also says, "Let your

---

667. *Pirkei Avos* 3:21. See also Rav Hirsch on *Pirkei Avos* 3:21.
668. Rambam, *Commentary on Mishnah, Niddah* 5:6.
669. *Proverbs* 4:22.
670. *Pirkei Avos* 6:7.

house be a meeting place for the wise men. Sit at the dust of their feet and drink their words thirstily,"[671] and "He who does not study the Torah deserves death."[672] The Gemara tells us, "Greater is the study of Torah than the rebuilding of the Temple,"[673] and "Even at the hour of death, a man should immerse himself in the study of Torah."[674] Rabbeinu Bachya says, "Man was created for Torah study" and "Engage in the study of Torah and its commandments, and you will merit redemption."[675] The Ramchal says that "Every aspect of the creation is rectified through Torah study."[676] None of this should diminish the value of good deeds, as the Talmud says, "Torah study is greater because it leads to practice"[677] and "The world stands on three things: Torah, prayer, and acts of kindness."[678] The Ramban says, "Be careful to study the Torah diligently, so that you will fulfill it. And when you rise from your studies, look into what you have learned to see what words you can fulfill."[679] Rav Hirsch says, "You must study for practical life--that is the fundamental principle of the law. With attentive mind and with receptive heart you must study in order to practice. You must aim at learning from the law a way of life, which is its true teaching; only then can you learn it properly, only then will it disclose to you its inmost meaning."[680] However, the inestimable value of Torah study, in part due to its power to bring us

---

671. *Pirkei Avos* 1:2.
672. *Pirkei Avos* 1:13.
673. *Megillah* 16b.
674. *Shabbos* 83b.
675. *Kad HaKemach, Torah.*
676. *Derech Hashem* 4:2:4.
677. *Kiddushin* 45b.
678. *Pirkei Avos* 1:2.
679. *Igeres HaRamban.*
680. *Horeb* 493.

to do good deeds, should be indisputable.

The prohibition against *bitul Torah* does not mean that one must study every second but that one should not waste an opportunity to study. For example, legitimate attempts to earn a living[681] or activities to preserve one's health and mind[682] are not considered *bitul Torah*. The ideal measure of Torah study is difficult to gauge; nevertheless, *bitul Torah* is a grave sin. The Chofetz Chaim explains:

> There is no end to the eternal reward for this commandment, as it is equal in weight to all of the other commandments combined, as explained in the Mishnah in *Peah* (1:1). The Talmud Yerushalmi (*Peah* 1:1) says, "All of the commandments are not equal to one word of Torah study." Conversely, the penalty for *bitul Torah* is equal to that of all the other commandments combined. As our Rabbis say (*Chagiga* 1:7),"The Holy One overlooked idol worship, immorality, and the spilling of blood, but He did not overlook *bitul Torah*."[683]

The Chofetz Chaim adds that the obligation in Torah study is not

---

681. *Sefer Chofetz Chaim, Pesicha, Asean,* 12.
682. *Horeb* 495: Rav Hirsch says, "Certainly you should take recreation, since recreation belongs to the duties which you owe to your mental and physical powers. But let your recreation itself be useful to your body, your mind and your spirit; and the more useful it is, the nobler and the worthy of yourself you will be." He says also, "It is your duty to fill your heart and mind with the waters of the Torah...." and, "God will demand a reckoning for every moment of your time."
683. *Sefer Chofetz Chaim, Pesicha, Asean,* 12. The Vilna Goan says that each word of Torah study is counted as a mitzvah in itself (*Sh'nos Eliyahu, Peah* 1:1).

based on a man's level of learning or comprehension of material. A man may learn according to his ability with materials that are understandable to him.[684]

As explained earlier, a woman's connection to *Limud Torah* is through support of the learning of the people around her.[685] Many Torah authorities of our times call for women to learn practical halachah and *mussar* and philosophy on Torah values and behavior. However, this is not considered part of the commandment of *Limud Torah*.[686] Rather, the deep internal connection between husband and wife makes it so that the husband's divine reward for *Limud Torah* is equally shared by the wife if she enables his learning.[687]

What happens if the wife does not enable her husband's learning, Heaven forbid, or on a subtle level discourages it? As the Mishnah says, "According to the work is the reward."[688] The wife's assistance is what produces her reward. Rav Yaakov Wolfe points out that the "greater promise" that the Gemara describes as being given to women results from the women's support of their husband's and children's Torah learning. The Gemara which describes this "greater promise" subsequently describes the wife's support of learning. As Rav Wolfe writes, "*Chazal* say, 'Greater is the promise that Hashem made to women than that made to men.' And what is the merit [behind this promise]? 'They bring their children to the house of books.

---

684. *Sefer Chofetz Chaim, Pesicha, Asean,* 12.
685. *Berachos* 17a; Rav Yonasan Eivishitz, *Yaros Davash, Drasha* 1; See also Chapter Seven.
686. *Mishneh Torah, Hilchos Talmid Torah* 1:1; *Takufa U'Baiyoseha,* p. 279. See also Rav Moshe Sternbuch, *Moadim U'Zmanim,* vol. 1, *siman* 2.
687. *Derek Pekudecha, Hakdamah,* 9:4; See also Chapter Nine.
688. *Pirkei Avos* 5:23.

They encourage their husbands and their sons to learn Mishnah in the house of study. They look for their husbands to travel to different cities to learn Torah, and they look for their husbands to return from the house of study.' "[689]

The problem is the false teachings of women's higher spirituality may cause attitudes that serve as an automatic discouragement to the husband's learning. Firstly, a wife who regards *Limud Torah* as something the husband alone needs to lift himself to her level sends a very different message than the wife who admires the husband for his unique and intrinsic abilities. The first attitude is embarrassing; the second is inspiring. The Steipler Rav is reported to have said that the single biggest cause for failure in the learning of yeshiva students is a lack of respect and honor for the students. And as Rav Yoel Schwartz has written, even adults need positive recognition.[690] Rav Schwartz applies to this idea the Talmudic story of Choni Hamaagal who returned to the local *bais hamidrash* after sleeping for seventy years. When the people in the *bais hamidrash* failed to recognize him and give him the honor of years before, he cried out "a companion or death."[691]

Some people have tried to argue that a wife's admiration for her husband's hard work will generate sufficient respect. However, that argument seems naive to human nature. Whether it be wrong or right, honor more commonly flows to those with the highest abilities, not to those who try the hardest. A wife may enable the husband to have free time for learning and she may even speak encouragingly of his learning, but her efforts may be seriously undermined if she regards him as less the capa-

---

689. *Takufa U'Baiyoseha*, p. 279 (Rav Yaakov Wolfe, b. 19th century, a key figure in the Bais Yaakov system).
690. *The Eternal Jewish Home*, pp. 44-45.
691. *Taanis* 23a.

ble man off to do important work and more the spiritually deficient being who needs to fix himself up with spiritual medicine.

Secondly, the view of Torah learning as nothing other than a medicine for the sick could discourage many women from wanting to support it more than a token amount. Again, this is human nature. People want to be part of important and productive projects.[692] A woman is far more inclined to dedicate herself to enabling Torah learning if she views it as a contribution to herself, her family, and the world (which of course it is). Teachings about the greatness of Torah to the world are negated in psychological ways when Torah learning is viewed as just something one's husband needs to fix himself. (As shown before, a man's obligation in Torah learning is very much a function of elevated qualities of his spiritual makeup.)

Thirdly, the men themselves may be discouraged by this view of Torah strictly as spiritual medicine for themselves. As the *Meom Loaz* tells us, the Torah offers man a variety of views on himself. Sometimes the man is told, "the gnat was created before you."[693] And sometimes the man is told, "you were created before the angels."[694] A person cannot always motivate himself by concentrating on his or her deficiencies. As Rav Moshe Feinstein tells us, "When a person views himself as inferior, he tells himself that he will not be able to understand Torah. Therefore, he does not even begin to study and does not take action to do good deeds."[695] Mind you, women should also not be told to view their responsibilities strictly from the angle of personal deficiency. For example, the preference for the wife to

---

692. *Chayi Olam* 1:5.
693. *Sanhedrin* 38.
694. *Meam Loez, Bereishis* 1:27.
695. *Derosh Moshe, Hakdamah*, p. 11, as translated by R. Zelig Pliskin in *Consulting the Wise*.

perform the candle lighting[696] on Shabbos is a function of the woman's differing connections to that mitzvah and can be viewed in more than one way. On one hand, her lighting the candles is an atonement for the sin of Chava.[697] On the other hand, it is a fitting addition to her activities as caretaker of the home.[698] To view it entirely from the angle of deficiency can be debilitating, even if on a subtle level, particularly for the people of our generation.

One should not think that this discouragement to learning works strictly on a subtle level. In many cases, it functions quite conspicuously and to much harm. But even the subtle influences take an enormous toll. The benefits of Torah learning on one's *yiras shemayim* do not diminish in the course of one's learning. As the Gemara teaches, the review of something one hundred times does not compare to the review of something one hundred and one times.[699]

Similarly, excellence in Torah depends on intense commitment. As the Rambam says, "The Rabbis taught that the Torah can only be fully comprehended by those who "kill themselves over it."[700] The Chazon Ish said, "Diligent toil is the most desired ingredient [in study]."[701] It is said that the Steipler Rav often responded to requests for blessings of success in learning

---

696. *Shulchan Aruch, Orach Chaim* 263; *Mishnah Berurah* 263:11.
697. *Talmud Yerushalmi, Shabbos* 2:6: "How do we know of the commandment of candle lighting [with respect to women]? She extinguished the light of the world, as it is written, 'The candle of the Lord is the soul of man' (*Mishlei* 20:27). Therefore, she should fulfill the commandment of candlelighting."
698. *Shulchan Aruch, Orach Chaim* 263; *Mishnah Berurah* 263:11; *Halichos Bas Yisrael* 1:15.
699. *Chagigah* 9b as explained by *Rashi*.
700. *Mishneh Torah, Hilchos Talmud Torah* 1:8-10.
701. Chazon Ish, *Kovetz Igeres* 1:1.

by stressing the value of one's commitment to learning. He would offer his blessings for success and stress that success comes through distancing oneself from *bitul Torah*.[702]

There are abundant stories which emphasize this point. In one story told in *For Love of Torah*, Rav Chaim Schmulevitz tells of his visit to this uncle's yeshiva in Lithuania where he asked his uncle, Rav Avraham Yoffen, to show him the most outstanding student in the yeshiva. Rav Yaffen pointed out various students and offered different praises of each of them. One student was called deeply thinking, another was broad in knowledge, and another was clever. When Rav Schmulevitz asked which was the most outstanding, his uncle turned towards a student studying in the corner of the room. He said that this student was not presently the deepest or the most knowledgeable, but he is the greatest *mevakesh*, or seeker. He said also that the student studies with sincere spiritual yearning for the word of Hashem, and eventually he will outpace the others. That student was Yaakov Yisrael Kanievsky, who was known many years later as the Steipler Goan and recognized as one of the *Gedolei HaDor*.[703]

Another story takes place in Lithuania before the war. A *baal habayis* was seen by his neighbors hurrying toward the study hall on the morning after Shavuos. Since the *baal habayis* had spent the entire night before studying as is customary on Shavuos, his friends took notice of his returning so soon to study. When one man asked if the *baal habayis* was not satisfied for now, the *baal habayis* replied, "Have you ever heard a drunk say that he has had enough to drink?"[704]

In addition to the portrayal of one man's enthusiasm for

---

702. *For Love of Torah*, p. 164.
703. *For Love of Torah*, pp. 109-110.
704. *For Love of Torah*, p. 110.

study, the forgoing story points out another important idea as well. Sometimes the call for Torah study is obvious and its fulfillment manageable. Other times excuses for not studying make themselves readily available. Subtle influences, like the attitude of one's community and family, often make the difference when the scales are evenly balanced between *Limud Torah* and *bitul Torah*.[705] Every man is regularly faced with a multitude of dramatic moments where he could just as well learn Torah or not learn Torah. Success in these moments, or many of them, is a key ingredient in serious long-term growth.

Naturally, we should all struggle to never be the cause of *bitul Torah* by others, Heaven forbid. On this matter, a story is told in *For Love of Torah* of a European Jew who visited the Steipler Rav in Eretz Yisrael. The Steipler read the man's name from his *kvittel*[706] and asked him if he had a brother living in a certain neighborhood in Eretz Yisrael. The Steipler who had never before met either the man before him nor the brother asked that the brother come to meet him. When the brother came, the Steipler asked him if it was his custom to study at a certain *bais hamidrash* on Friday afternoons. The Steipler asked him as well if he recalled being disturbed by an elderly *shamash*[707] who forced him to move his seat as the *shamash* cleaned around it. The man responded affirmatively to both questions. The Steipler told him that the *shamash* appeared to him in a dream and said that he has no peace in the next world because of the *bitul Torah* he caused. And so the Steipler asked

---

705. The foregoing story is not brought to say that not rushing to the study hall on Shavuos day is always considered *bitul Torah*. Many factors must be considered for such a determination.
706. A written request for the utterance of prayers. It contains the Jewish names of the subjects of the prayers.
707. A person who attends to the upkeep of a synagogue.

the man to visit the grave of the *shamash* and grant him forgiveness so that he may be given peace.[708]

Indeed, we should all fear ever being a hindrance to someone's Torah learning or to any of the other aspects of *Avodas Hashem* discussed here. On this danger, Rav Hirsch issues the sternest of warnings:

> Parents, teachers, brothers and sisters, friends and all of you who exert influence by deed and by the written or spoken word, on young souls — they are blind of mind and their minds are illumined by the light of your mind; what you, by your word and example, tell them to be true and good will be regarded by them as true and good for a long time, and they will base their life on it until they are able to judge for themselves. Do not put a stumbling-block into their path. Woe to them if you are not honest with them, if you present to them false doctrine as the truth, evil as good, falsehood as truth, if you turn night into day and the daylight of truth into darkness. One day they will awake and curse you, and God will hear that curse! Fear Him, if you do not fear human beings--He sees into your hearts....Woe to you, woe if even one single human soul accuses you before the Supreme Judge's Throne of having stolen, not his honour, peace, or pleasure, but God and morality and thus crushed the life out of his life![709]

It is easy sometimes for an older person to forget the vulnerabilities of young people. By analogy, we all know how to get to our houses, but forget sometimes that visitors need careful directions lest they get lost. To the one who has made the trip it all seems

---

708. *For Love of Torah,* p. 179.
709. *Horeb* 383-385.

so simple. You drive for a few minutes and make a left. If you have been there, such directions may get you home, if not, they may take you to a bad neighborhood. Our generation may need special care in this regard since the influence of secular culture has left us, to continue the metaphor, with poor senses of direction in social matters. One cannot be sloppy in the teaching of these essential principles and cannot take for granted the ignorance and vulnerability of youth. As a side note, *baalei tshuvah* are most vulnerable because of their typical openness to the new world they have encountered. They are told in most cases to forget the teachings of their past and absorb the new ones of the Torah. Educators must be careful as to what is transmitted as being Torah because these hungry souls absorb the teachings of the teachers much as children do those of their parents. And the foundations of one's youth are difficult to remove.[710]

---

710. See *Pirkei Avos* 4:20; *Mishneh Torah, Hilchos Maamarim* 3:3; *Horeb* 382.

Conclusion

"Taste and see that the Lord is good; Happy is the person who takes refuge in Him."[711]

This book, in its discussion of the roles and natures of men and women, has presented and explained classical sources and critiqued some modern treatments of the subject. A remaining question of how to present the material to students is not a simple matter, since every student is different. Hopefully, one accomplishment of this book has been a laying out of boundaries on what statements are improper to make regardless of one's estimation of a student's needs. Hopefully, suggestions for productive presentation of these subjects can be found here as well.

As a side note, the author should say that he can likewise not

---

711. *Tehillim* 34:9.

claim to have the hold on the truth, not by any means, but can attest to his attempt to research these matters from multiple angles and to report his findings without conscious manipulation. Readers will have to judge for themselves about these subjects and are encouraged to review the numerous sources brought here. If they do, then the most important accomplishment of this book will be to have presented a breadth of material from which a person can come to more informed understandings on these subjects.

In the spirit of the goals of this book, it may be useful to summarize some of the arguments of the book and to present a general check list of sorts for presentation of these subjects. Naturally, such a summary is a simplification of the many aspects of these subjects, but it nevertheless may help to put approaches to material into a practical framework.

The summary is as follows: Men and women are both created in Hashem's divine love[712] and wisdom.[713] Both have been created in Hashem's image[714] and are irreplaceable as agents in Hashem's holy mission on this earth.[715] Hashem purposely created men and women with different roles and natures so as to arrange for a harmony in their coming together. It is a team of players with different skills.[716] A fundamental dynamic of that specialization in skills is that the man is the more direct agent in the general spreading of Torah values to the world and the

---

712. *Tehillim* 145:9; *Derech Hashem* 1:2:1. See chapter one.
713. *Moreh Nevuchim* 3:20; *Chovos HaLevavos, Shaar HaBitachon* 2-3-2.
714. *Bereishis* 1:27; *Pirkei Avos* 3:14; Rav Hirsch on *Bereishis* 5:2. See chapter three.
715. Rav Hirsch on *Bereishis* 5:2.
716. *Judaism Eternal*, vol. II, pp. 63-64. See chapter four.

woman is the invaluable helpmate[717] or the behind the scenes person in that effort.[718] An analogy might be the President and the Secretary of State of the United States.

Western culture tends to devalue modesty and behind the scenes contribution, so the preciousness of the woman's role is often overlooked by people.[719] Similarly, Western culture in its recent manifestations tends to put inordinate pressures on men, so the enjoyment of the man's role is often overlooked by people. A person must know that true happiness[720] and eternal reward[721] come only through living in accordance with Hashem's plan.

The man in his more direct role in the spreading of Torah is obligated[722] in some commandments from which the woman is exempt. Generally speaking, the reasons for the exemption transcend human logic.[723] This transcendence of logic is not a push-off to our inquiry but a feature of a life system which develops well-rounded people and true servants of Hashem.[724]

However, one may say as well that the woman is exempt to enable her to excel in her role as helpmate.[725] A single woman is

---

717. *Bereishis* 2:18; *Akeidas Yitzchok, Bereishis, shaar* 9: 7-8.
718. *Judaism Eternal*, vol. II, p. 51.
719. See chapter four.
720. *Mishlei* 3:17; *Pirkei Avos* 4:1.
721. *Pirkei Avos* 4:2, 4:13, 3:18, and 6:7; *Koheles* 12:16.
722. *Kiddushin* 29a.
723. *Igeres Moshe, Orach Chaim* IV, 49. See also *Kasav Sofer, She'elos U'Tshuvos, Orach Chaim, Tshuvah* 75.
724. See *Michtav MeEliyahu,* 1:218:220. See chapter six.
725. *Sefer Abudraham, Seder Tefillas shel Chol, Birchas HaMitzvos U'Mishpatim; Malmid HaTalmidim, Parshas Lech Lecha;* Ritva and *Tosfos HaRid* (*Torah Temimah, Shemos* 13:9); Rashbatz, *Magen Avos* 2:6; and many others. See chapter seven.

exempt to encourage her to get married.[726] There are other reasons as well and maybe we can summarize them best by saying as follows: men are obligated in commandments because of special qualities of men,[727] and women are exempt from these commandments and enable men to perform them because of special qualities of women.[728] Perhaps the summary can be phrased as well by saying that men excel in performing the positive time-bound commandments, and women excel in enabling others to perform those commandments.

On this last idea of the special qualities of men and women, it should be worth adding that our abilities should never be used for self-glorification. As the Mishnah says, "All that the Holy one created in His world, He created for His glory."[729] The Ramban says as follows:

> And for what should man have a proud heart. If he is wealthy, Hashem causes poverty and wealth. If he is given honor, is not [all honor] from Hashem. As it says, "wealth and honor come from you."[730] And how can he pride himself on honor due to his Creator? And if he takes pride in his wisdom [Hashem] removes the speech of the able and the wisdom of the aged.[731] It

---

726. Rav Shlomo Aaron Wertheimer, *Divrei Shlomo* (beginning) found in the back of the *Abudraham HaShalaim*, (Jerusalem: 5723), p. 405. See also *Tziunim L'Torah*, *clal* 39. See chapter seven.

727. *Tiferes Yisrael* 4; *Zies Ra'anan* (*Magen Avraham*) on *Shmuel* 1:1:13. See chapter twelve.

728. Rav Hirsch on *Vayikra* 23:43; *Yabia Omer* 40:9. See chapter eight.

729. *Pirkei Avos* 6:11.

730. *Divrei HaYamim* 1:29:12.

731. *Iyov* 12:20.

appears that all people are equal before God. In His
fury, He casts down the arrogant.[732]

Concerning the possession of wisdom, the Ramchal says, "There
is no place for haughtiness and boasting over one's wisdom.
Rather, a person is obligated to assist those who are in need of
it."[733] Concerning wealth he says, "One who is wealthy may
rejoice in his portion, but he is obligated to help those who are
indigent."[734] We can reason that wealth, in addition to its most
commonly recognized form of financial wealth, is manifested as
well in numerous other forms, including physical and emotional
health, intelligence, and spiritual sensitivity.[735]

And we must remember as well not only the needs of each
of our fellows, but the specialness and unique qualities of each
as well. As the verse teaches us, "God made man in His image,
in the image of God He created him, Male and female He created them." Upon this verse, the Mishnah says, "Beloved is man,
for he was created in the image [of Hashem]. And it was out of
special fondness that this was made known to him."[736] And once
again, the Midrash says, "I call heaven and earth to witness
be...man or woman...only according to their actions will the spirit of holiness rest upon them."[737]

_____

732. *Igeres HaRamban.*
733. *Mesillas Yishaarim* 22.
734. *Mesillas Yishaarim* 22.
735. According to Rav Hirsch, the Torah's command for the gracious
     acceptance of strangers and the protection of widows and
     orphans extends to "every dependent person." In other words,
     dependency assumes many forms, and the obligation to share our
     blessings with our brethren is multifaceted. (*Horeb* 379).
736. *Pirkei Avos* 3:18.
737. *Seder Eliyahu Rabbah* 9. Also brought by *Judaism Eternal*, vol.
     II, p. 96.

The foregoing is a simple summary, but the author has found that it often serves well as a workable approach to the subject for many people. More complex views on each of these points can be found in the classical sources referenced and briefly described on these pages and in other sources referenced in the many books of our Sages.

Indeed, the Torah is a vast sea, easily large enough for us to swim in all our lives and never find cause to leave it, Heaven forbid. As has been said throughout this book, the Torah is the instruction book to the best life for ourselves. A person will only succeed if he or she struggles for growth with Torah as his or her guiding light. David HaMelech assured us of the following, "Hashem is close to all who call upon Him, who call upon Him in truth."[738] The world may look strangely on the Jews for our adherence to the Torah, the source of truth, but this is a sad reflection on the world, not on us. As Akavyah ben Mehalel said, "Better for me to be regarded as a fool all of my days than to be evil for one moment in the eyes of Hashem."[739] And, "The essence of the matter is that all is heard. Fear God and do His commandments; because that is the sum of the person."[740]

---

738. *Tehillim* 145.
739. *Eduyos* 5:6.
740. *Koheles* 12:13.